EVOLUTION OF
FAITH

EVOLUTION OF FAITH

PHILIP S. RADCLIFFE

Evolution of Faith

Copyright © 2023 by Philip S. Radcliffe. All rights reserved.

No part of this publication may be reproduced, stored in a retrieval system or transmitted in any way by any means, electronic, mechanical, photocopy, recording or otherwise without the prior permission of the author except as provided by USA copyright law.

The opinions expressed by the author are not necessarily those of URLink Print and Media.

1603 Capitol Ave., Suite 310 Cheyenne, Wyoming USA 82001
1-888-980-6523 | admin@urlinkpublishing.com

URLink Print and Media is committed to excellence in the publishing industry.

Book design copyright © 2023 by URLink Print and Media. All rights reserved.

Published in the United States of America

Library of Congress Control Number: 2023900983
ISBN 978-1-68486-348-8 (Paperback)
ISBN 978-1-68486-351-8 (Digital)

19.12.22

Contents

Introduction 7
Hunter Gatherers 11
Cognitive Development 18
The Agricultural Revolution 21
Monotheistic Evangelism 32
Literate Revolution 38
Beginnings of Democracy 45
Industrial Revolution 1865–1945 49
Atomic Age 1945–2000 56
Information Age 2000– 62
Bibliography 83

Introduction

Evolution and faith are two terms not generally mentioned together since Neo-Darwinism claimed that evolution replaced religious belief as the singular driving force behind the development of society. The famous Scopes Trial won a place for evolution in the hearts and minds of Americans even though Scopes, a high school teacher, was found guilty and fined for teaching evolution in Tennessee in 1925. In passing, his verdict was set aside on appeal and the Butler Act, under which he was tried, was repealed in 1967. Evolution is generally acknowledged to be an observed fact; however, the extent and pervasiveness of its effects are still debated within the scientific community.

Selective breeding in the past improved agricultural production of meat, dairy products, and eggs. Today with the genome identified as a driver of change and modification, genetic engineering is a significant factor in human health as well as agricultural production. Dr. Francis Collins, a geneticist and director of the successful human genome decoding effort at NIH, wrote a book, *The Language of God*, wherein he proposed that DNA and genetics could well be the vehicle an all-powerful Creator employed to achieve His goal of developing humanity in His "image and likeness."

In my previous writing on faith, and Christian faith in particular, I proposed that in my opinion, science and Christian faith were not in opposition but rather enjoyed a symbiosis strengthening each. My second book dealt with how an individual's faith was formed and how I believed faith interacted with life. It is my objective in this writing to explore how humanity discovered faith and evolved it into a course of conduct that can be developed, observed, and practiced today.

Covering subjects as broad as the history of the species and the development of religious faith requires some degree of hubris. Fortunately, I can discuss the subject and still claim some humility by citing as inspiration three works, two by authors that know and respect each other. *Sapiens: A Brief History of Humankind* by Yuval Noah Hurari and *The World Until Yesterday* by Jared Diamond. I have previously read and recall with admiration Diamond's two other seminal works: *Guns, Germs and Steel* and *Collapse*. The first book provided a basis for western dominance in today's world economy, and the second reviewed how and why societies expand and collapse. Mr. Hurari is a history professor in Israel, and Jared Diamond is an anthropologist. This might explain at some level their differences in approach and variation in conclusions. The third book is a major tome of over 1,100 pages written by Diarmaid MacCulloch, *Christianity: The First Three Thousand Years*. Dr. MacCulloch is a professor of the History of the Church at Oxford University and a prize-winning author on history and the Church.

In my previous writing, I pointed out that in 1959 I graduated from college on a Sunday and started working for IBM the following Monday. In college, I studied liberal arts and included courses in accounting, economics, and business administration. Liberal arts included concentrations in history and political science . My academic background was in history while my occupational experience of over forty years has been in computer science and the application of computers in the engineering dominated field of real time data acquisition and control of industrial processes. I note this to explain both my empathy with and appreciation for the differences a historian and a more scientific approach of an anthropologist might yield. A historian is more likely in my experience to study a topic for some time, develop conclusions, and then review the topic selecting examples that fit one conclusions. A scientist is trained to carefully observe and note all observations, returning later to either draw inference from the observations or merely highlight tendencies or differences.

Unfortunately, as I completed reading the works of the first two esteemed academics, I became disappointed in the messages with which both writers concluded their works. Mr. Hurari moved into a discussion of almost e picurean proportions pointing out the measures humanity pursued in trying to define pleasure in our existence where pleasure was not a denial of sensory pursuit nor did it confine itself to a total pursuit of sensory pleasure. There was little to no attention given to any discussion of purpose, faith, or any eternal veritas. In his concluding chapters, Mr. Diamond lapsed into humanity's downfall due to poor dietary habits, particularly salt and sugar. I must admit in these two cases I felt engaged in their preliminaries but disappointed in the conclusions which struck me as prosaic when considering the promise of their titles. The third work is definitely more of a challenge to wade through and absorb, at least in part. *Christianity: The First Three Thousand Years* looks at the march of Christian beliefs from its roots in Judaism through several transitions at various points of the globe in various periods of time.

As the focus of this work moves toward today's observations and experiences, I will draw more directly on the series of readings I have been engaged in while seeking to address issues relating to science, religion, and consciousness. With this as introduction, let us now go back to the beginning of man's presence on the third rock from the sun.

Hunter Gatherers

Yuval Noah Hurari pointed out a relatively new fact brought out by the collection of DNA in a massive database illustrating the migration of our species, *Homo sapiens*, since its introduction at the horn of Africa some 50,000 to 100,000 years ago. Analysts discovered in 2010 that from 1% to 4% of DNA among people with European genetic backgrounds can be traced to Neanderthal sources. Neanderthals represent one branch of hominoid that existed from around two hundred thousand years ago to about thirty thousand years ago. You will note that there was a period of at least ten thousand years, allowing for transport delays, getting out of Africa when both *Homo sapiens* (Cro-Magnon) and *Homo* Neanderthal overlapped in Europe. For some time, given the evidence of a Neanderthal skeleton with bones that appeared to be damaged by a weapon, it was believed that the Neanderthals and sapiens evidently engaged in conflict and the sapiens won to the point of exterminating the Neanderthals. The new DNA evidence points to a higher probability that sapiens bred with Neanderthals and eventually outreproduced Neanderthal to the point of extinction.

During this period from around forty thousand to thirty thousand years ago both Neanderthals and sapiens were hunter gatherers and there was adequate space for each group to survive on game over a wide area including all of Eurasia. What is now speculated, based on what evidence archeology yields to date, is that sapiens more social behavior enabled them to absorb several other hominoid species in Europe, Asia, Southeast Asia, and Africa. Thus, while natural selection may have favored earlier species or subspecies in terms of survival within geographic regions, when *Homo sapiens* moved out of the horn of Africa and joined local hominoids already in residence, they successfully produced hybrid species that have most physiology and biochemistry in common among sapiens yet have unique characteristics that seem favored within their region. As examples of this theory, Northern Europeans generally have fairer complexions and tend to be taller, characteristics of Neanderthal precedents, while Southeast Asians could represent hybridization between sapiens and *Homo floresiensis* bands of darker skinned hominoids who only measured to around 3.5 feet in height.

In today's world, we have the species *Homo sapiens* that have in common, physiology and biochemistry while still possessing unique physical features by region and race. However, the origin of the human species now is believed to go back beyond *Homo sapiens* and back beyond the Neanderthals of perhaps two hundred thousand years ago. Evidence in Tanzania indicates that some member of *Homo erectus* engaged in hunting and consuming their prey as long as two million years ago, or about four hundred ninety-eight million years before the Cambrian explosion. We have significant evidence that the post Cambrian Neanderthals used tools, buried their dead, and engaged in apparent ritual practices at least on some occasions. There are very limited evidence or observable remains from hominoids preceding the Neanderthals. During this whole period, it is acknowledged that hominoids and their human successors survived as hunter gatherers, over a range of at least one million years and perhaps as long as two million years.

I will attempt some analysis of spiritual characteristics either evidenced in archeological observations or hypothesized from characteristics observed in "traditional" societies. Traditional society is a term coined by Jared Diamond and includes primitive cultures in remote areas of the globe as they existed in an undisturbed environment that was documented in the 1930s and before.

Before we attempt any analysis, let us look into a brief history of what preceded hominoid presence two million years ago. This look back into the creation of the earth will be brief and is employed to put the history of humans into perspective. Based on carbon dating and mathematical modeling of the creation of our solar system, including what sampling we have done on the moon and mars, it has been generally accepted in the scientific community that the earth is about 4.5 billion years old. Dated fossil records indicate that there was water covering much of the planet as early as about 4.25 billion years ago. In the period from 4.25 billion years to around 2 billion years ago there is fossil evidence of single celled bacterial cells and archaeal cells that reproduced as clones and did gather in colonies as fungal colonies or bacterial colonies where each cell existed independently without any nucleus or mitochondria. Around 3.5 billion years ago prokaryotes that lived in colonies seemed to have developed photosynthesis thus adding oxygen to our atmosphere. Somewhere around 2 billion years ago eukaryote cells were found in fossils. Theoretically, eukaryotes came about as a single symbiotic combination among archaeal and bacterial cells. Eukaryotic cells have nuclei, mitochondria, and DNA and are the basis for all complex life forms. In the period from two billion years ago until about five hundred million years ago life existed as sponges and other simple life forms in addition to bacteria and archaeal cells. The Cambrian explosion occurred about five hundred million years ago and is evident in myriad new species appearing in the fossil record in multiple locations simultaneously or almost simultaneously.

In the period from five hundred million years ago to about four million years ago various plants, fish, reptiles, and mammals appeared and existed, again based on fossil records which change from time to time as new discoveries are made. Then about 3.6 million years ago, *Homo Australopithecus Afarensis* left human-like foot prints on volcanic ash in Laetoli, Kenya. From fragmented remains, the species had an anterior projecting face, smaller canines and molars then any of the great apes and apparently existed as a scavenger including meat in its diet. *Homo erectus* appears in Africa about two million years ago and probably includes "cousins" such as *Homo georgicus, Homo pekinensis and Homo heidelbergensis*. These hominoids developed early weapons such as primitive spears and stone axes, hunting skills, the ability to travel significant distances and control fire. *Homo erectus* had a brain about 75% the size of modern humans, while the predecessor, Australopithecus had a brain size of less than 50% of the size of modern humans. It has been theorized that it was the carnivorous appetite with a high concentration of protean in meat that evolved increased brain capacity.

The preceding is a highly condensed and abbreviated representation of the evolution of the planet earth and life upon it as compiled from my readings of cosmologists, anthropologists, archeologists, physicists, historians, and other members of the academic and scientific community. This account does not detail events such as the apparent diminution of oxygen that occurred about 2.25 million years ago and several ice ages and periods of greater than usual warmth occurring in cycles over the 4.5 billion years covered. What all accounts, that I have read, agree upon is that there are several occasions of events over this extended period of history that are not readily explainable or predictable. Science continues to explore these gaps and from time to time there are new breakthroughs but there is significant probability that some ancient mysteries will only have unproven hypothetical solutions that will be able to be modeled on a theoretical basis but not replicated.

For purposes of this discussion let us assume that the origins and evolution as presented are valid. Remember that my subject is the evolution of faith and that subject only begins with the presence of a self-aware being and that surely starts with *Homo sapiens* a hundred thousand years ago and perhaps earlier with Neanderthals up to three hundred thousand years ago. These early humans left evidence of their existence in cave drawings, burials, and remnants of their communal existence. From these archeological finds, we have been able to form pictures of their existence and daily life patterns. The descriptions of these primitive humans' activities have been reinforced by anthropological observations of "traditional" societies that were isolated from the development of modern society.

Based upon this fragmented evidence, we can generalize on humanity's survival as hunter gatherers for at least the period from as long ago as three hundred thousand years ago to around fifteen thousand years ago when evidence has been found indicating that domestication of some animals began. By 9,000 BCE (Before the Christian Epic), eleven thousand years ago, Jericho emerged as a settlement and the era of human survival exclusively as hunter gatherers was ending, except in the isolated "traditional society" cases. The generalizations that I have read and seem to me to be at least reasonable include:

- Hunter gatherer societies are organized in small groups where each member knows all or at least almost all of the other members.
- Hunter gatherers are nomadic, moving through familiar territory as seasons changed, and the range of their prey adjusted to the season.
- In most cases, bands of hunter gatherers knew their territorial limits and had limited contact with abutting neighbors.
- Observation of traditional societies suggests that care of and regard for elders varied from respect for elder wisdom and therefore regard for elder care, to elimination of aging members and spouses as drags on the band's ability to efficiently secure food.
- There is evidence in the archeological records that some bands had within their group persons regarded as having ability to heal, predict, effect the environment, or communicate with spirits.

When dealing with generalizations about this period, humanity's ability to communicate was very limited. Again, anthropologists note that in traditional societies languages were very local, and bands might know the vocabulary of their neighbor but not the language of bands or tribes one neighbor removed. In areas where the local environment supported game sufficient to maintain generally good food supplies, territories were quite small. However, in arid areas, high altitude areas, or extremely cold areas where territory needed to be extensive and hunting was difficult and gathering plant food from the wild was similarly a challenge, a band's territory was usually quite extensive. In all cases, vocabulary when observed was quite limited and generally involved commands for cooperative action, warnings, and personal requests such as food, warmth, or sex.

These generalizations were a basis for Professor Hurari's thesis that one reason for *Homo sapiens* success was an ability to gossip as language skills and brain size increased. He reasoned that this characteristic enlarged the sphere of contacts sapiens could encounter without the same level of intimate personal contact required within a band or tribe. "You and I could talk about them" and consequently, I would know how far to trust them. Again, several anthropological observations of traditional societies indicate that, as a percentage of total population, death rates from violence due to either fighting within the band or among the band and its neighbors was the major cause of adult death. It was noted that even during periods of major wars, modern societies did not have as high a death percentage from violence as that observed among tribes of hunter gatherers on a steady state basis. In the era of the hunter gatherer, strangers were considered as enemies to be killed either defensively or possibly as food.

Hunter gatherer population was small. Life was difficult and lived in the moment. History was for the most part irrelevant, except in the occasion of revenge, and forecasts were unknown. Language was limited and local in scope. Survival was the single theme of existence. Still, there is evidence that this new creature in what was already an ancient earth, questioned what was happening in his environment and why? In some individual burial sites, bodies were found with items interpreted as mystical components indicating that the individual had some apparent identification as a person with connections to perhaps a supernatural force. It is not until much later in time that we have evidence of any organized religion since there was no significant communal gathering in evidence. Humanity lived in bands and while there was apparently communal "ownership" of the band's territory there was no permanent settlement other than frequently visited sites such as caves or favored camp sites. Over time, there are indications that in some societies, bands began to ally with neighbors and formed larger cooperative groups to hunt larger game.

Perhaps the beginning of tribal structure and selection or election of societal leadership. Mystery was probably in evidence, but there is no indication of anything resembling faith.

This is the picture of humanity until sometime around 50,000 years ago or 48,000 BCE.

Cognitive Development

At 48,000 BCE, humanity still existed within the hunter-gatherer mode but significant changes in sophistication were beginning to be evident. Dinosaurs along with about half of all then existing animal species became extinct. *Homo erectus* had been using fire for warmth and protection for some time, but by about this time, cooking also became a standard use of fire. Also, clothing employing animal hides has been observed in the archeological record dating to this period.

A Hohle Fels flute dating from about 35,000 years ago was discovered in the cave of the same name in Germany in 2008 . In 2012, a new high-resolution carbon dating test indicated that flutes made from mute swan bone and woolly mammoth ivory found in the nearby Geisenklosterle cave dated back to forty-two thousand years ago. These flutes appear similar to today's recorder and suggest a beginning of another form of the arts and music, in addition to cave paintings. It has been suggested that this early music may have helped maintain bonds among larger groups of humans.

During this same Paleolithic period, decoration has been found on functional tools such as spear throwers, perforated batons, and lamps. Also, early sculpture including formed clay and carved stone has been found. The subjects of this prehistoric art include human figures, animals that were hunted as well as predators such as big cats, bears, and the woolly rhinoceros.

The presence of elements of the arts suggests larger gatherings developing as well as more permanent settlements in areas where game was generally available. For example, in Indonesia there is archeological evidence of an early permanent settlement as a fishing village. If these hypotheses are valid, this would suggest some collective pressure developing to insure a readily available supply of gathered plant food in such settlements.

This transition period extends from around fifty thousand years ago to around ten thousand years ago. The Neanderthals and eventually all the other hominoids, save sapiens, became extinct. However, sapiens continued to increase human population. It was during this period that humanity's cognitive development became evident based on archeological evidence. By cognitive development I refer to the awareness of surroundings and the development of a vocabulary sufficient to communicate this awareness to others in a nuanced and somewhat sophisticated manner. Art is one evidence of this cognitive ability both in terms of cave paintings and music.

There is no direct evidence of any specific theology or ritual practice from this period. However, the cognitive awareness of the total environment lends credence to the hypothesis that at least in individual bands or tribal groups, there were probably at least observances of some level of reverence to the supernatural. For example, in Sungir, Russia, according to Yuval Noah Harari, thirty-thousand-year-old gravesites were discovered in 1955 that showed a fifty five year old man and two sites belonging to a boy about twelve or thirteen and a girl of nine or ten. The bodies included extensive beading, ivory statuettes, and jewelry and other remnants that suggest at least status and perhaps reverence either for leadership or supernatural connection, including possible sacrifice. Similarly, some cave art suggests, through interpretation, possible depiction of spirits leaving bodies and potential worship of representative animals.

Most historians, anthropologists, and archeologists agree with the hypotheses that these earliest indications of belief in the supernatural were animistic and local to individual tribes. In his book *Understanding World Religions in 15 Minutes a Day*, Garry R. Morgan states this accepted position as follows: "I n human development animistic religions came first followed by polytheistic then monotheistic (and today by atheistic)." Mr. Morgan then characterizes animism as being passed along orally from generation to generation with no written scriptures or sacred writings. Also, there seems to be no expectation that people from other tribes or cultural groups were expected to serve the same spirits. In his analysis, Mr. Morgan asserts that all animists share certain common beliefs about the nature of the world, including:

- The world is full of spiritual beings which can be either figures in nature or ancestors;
- These spirit figures may be impersonal forces such as fate, or the evil eye, or combinations of all the above;
- Spirit figures are believed to have influence or control over people and events
- The animist goal is to determine what spirits are at work, so they can protect themselves and perhaps harness the power for their own benefit.

In his view, most animistic religions are pragmatic and focus on day-to-day matters rather than issues of eternal destiny or life after death. He points out that there are several situations where in contemporary practice, some Christians or other practicing religious members can still harbor animistic beliefs on day-to-day matters while holding to monotheism on longer term ethereal issues. For example, a black cat crossing one's path, an animistic observation, is considered to be bad luck by some practicing Christians.

The relationship of this period to faith and its evolution is essentially the starting point for the species having experienced cognitive awareness, coming to believe in some supernatural power or powers. It becomes evident in the next phase of human development that these inferred indications of belief become more expressed in the historical record and initiate the process of increasing sophistication.

The Agricultural Revolution

Thus far, we have commented on humanity's origin and organization into hunter-gatherer bands during a period extending from two million years ago to around fifty thousand years ago. At this point, indications were observed that established apparent cognition of the environment and an increasing population began to develop more social gatherings to improve the quality of what was still a very challenging lifestyle. The first transition ran from around fifty thousand years ago until around twelve thousand years ago, or around 10,000 BCE, when permanent settlements were initially observed in the historical record and plants and animals were domesticated. In the period around fifty thousand years ago, Paleolithic long stone tools were developed and in an approximate five- thousand-year window; modern homo-sapiens ancestors are now indicated to have cross bred with Neanderthals, Northern route Denisovans and, in a separate and apparently later occasion, Southern route Denisovans. The evidence for these separate hybridizing events includes DNA matching. Lack of Paleolithic tools in Southern route Denisovan cultures and extensive cultural distinctions that seem to reinforce this hypothesis.

We have found evidence that the initial animal to be domesticated was the dog who formed a symbiotic relationship, whereby man fed the dog from the successful fruits of the hunt. Goats, sheep, pigs, and cattle were all present in the Fertile Crescent covering modern Turkey, Iraq, and southwestern Iran from around 11,000 to 10,000 BCE. From there, both the use of domestic animals and planted crops migrated to Europe. Newly developed analysis and discrimination of ancient DNA samples have revealed new hypothesis of how the Agricultural Revolution came into being. Rather than hunter-gatherers discovering an improved way of life by cultivating their food instead of hoping to locate and kill it, the more socially developed Homo sapiens hybrids outreproduced and ultimately replaced the hunter-1gatherer nomadic tribes. This is the beginning of the Mesolithic and Epipaleolithic periods at the beginning of the Holocene (current) epoch. World population was estimated at between one and ten million people (the daytime population of Manhattan or less). Mesolithic cave drawings depicting war scenes and religious drawings have been discovered. Remains of the first stone structures have been uncovered in Jericho dating to 9,000 BCE. To be sure the Bronze Age was still more than six thousand years in the future and hunting and gathering were still practiced, but humanity had started to gather and raise part of its food supply to at least supplement hunting and gathering.

This period, from around 10,000 BCE until somewhere between 4,000 and 3,000 BCE, was still part of the Stone Age and farming "implements" were wooden and stone. By around 3,000 BCE, depending on what region of the world one is looking to, copper began to be observed. By this period, copper metallurgy was developing in Mesopotamia and cast copper tools and weapons dating to around 3,500 BCE have been found. This was the beginning of the Bronze Age when copper was alloyed with tin and the more useful and enduring bronze was employed in tools and weapons as well as an era where the wheel and ox drawn plow were employed to increase agricultural yield. By 1,000 BCE, the Iron Age emerged, and tools and weapons employed the new metal creating ever more productive and sophisticated possibilities. In 1974, Paolo Matthiae, an Italian archeologist, discovered one thousand eight hundredd complete clay tablets and an additional four thousand seven hundred tablet fragments. These tablets date to the period from 2,500 to 2,250 BCE, the height of the Bronze Age. The tablets were recorded in Sumerian and a previously unknown language that employed the Sumerian cuneiform script as a phonetic representation of a local Ebla language. A major subject was commerce, revealing Ebla as a major trade center and brewer of Ebla beer. Part of the subject matter of the tablets also included hymns, rituals, epics, and proverbs. Recall if you will that the genealogy in Genesis, according to the reckoning of young earth creationists, establishes the beginning of time in the Garden of Eden to around 4,000 BCE, making the earth about six thousand years old.

According to the b iblical account, Abraham from Ur in Mesopotamia, at age seventy-five proceeded with his barren wife Sarah, his nephew Lot, and other companions to the land of Canaan, between Syria and Egypt. There Abraham had a son Hagar by his wife's maidservant and then at age one hundred, a son with Sarah—Isaac, the heir of the promise. By cross correlating biblical references and recent archeological evidence as corroborated in another cache of thousands of ancient tablets found in a palace at Mari. It has been pretty well established that a migration occurred from Mughair, or Ur, a village two hundred miles southeast of Baghdad, around 2,000 BCE in the Bronze Age.

By this time in history, there is evidence of Hinduism in practice in India and Asia generally, animism in the Middle East, and the advent of monotheism in the Middle East. The animism of this period is difficult to distinguish between polytheism as it developed with the Greeks and Romans and the multiple idols worshipped in Hinduism, or the now more sophisticated animism with its collection of spirits. There is no question that by around four thousand years ago, humanity had developed beliefs, rituals, and some forms of corporate worship. Judaism had not yet developed into a theology but the earliest belief in a covenant with a Supreme Being had been initiated.

The following is a review of The Genesis Narrative in light of recent scholarship as prepared by the World History Center.

The saga of Abraham unfolds between two landmarks, the exodus from "Ur of the Chaldeans" (Ur Kasdim) of the family, or clan, of Terah and "the purchase of " (or "the burials in") the cave of Machpelah. Tradition seems particularly firm on this point. The Hebrew text, in fact, locates the departure specifically at Ur Kasdim, the Kasdim being none other than the Kaldu of the cuneiform texts at Mari. It is manifestly a migration of which one tribe is the center. The leader of the movement is designated by name: Terah, who "takes them out" from Ur, Abram his son, Lot the son of Haran, another son of Terah, and their wives, the best known being Sarai, the wife of Abram. The existence of another son of Terah, Nahor, who appears later, is noted.

> Most scholars agree that Ur Kasdim was the Sumerian city of Ur, today Tall al-Muqayyar (or Mughair), about 200 miles (300 km) southeast of Baghdad in lower Mesopotamia, which was excavated from 1922 to 1934. It is certain that the cradle of the ancestors was the seat of a vigorous polytheism whose memory had not been lost and whose uncontested master in Ur was Nanna (or Sin), the Sumero-Akkadian moon god. "They served other gods," Joshua, Moses' successor, recalled, speaking to their descendants at Shechem.
>
> After the migration from Ur (c. 2000 Bc), the reasons for which are unknown, the first important stopping place was Harran, where the caravan remained for some time. The city has been definitely located in upper Mesopotamia, between the Tigris and the Euphrates rivers, in the Balikh valley and can be found on the site of the modern Harran in Turkey. It has been shown that Harran was a pilgrimage city, for it was a center of the Sin cult and consequently closely related to the moon-god cult of Ur. The Mari tablets have shed new light on the patriarchal period, specifically in terms of the city of Harran.
>
> There have been many surprising items in the thousands of tablets found in the palace at Mari. Not only are the Hapiru ("Hebrews") mentioned but so also remarkably are the Banu Yamina ("Benjaminites"). It is not that the latter are identical with the family of Benjamin, a son of Jacob, but rather

that a name with such a biblical ring appears in these extra biblical sources in the 18th century Bc. What seems beyond doubt is that these Benjaminites (or Yaminites, meaning "Sons of the Right," or "Sons of the South," according to their habits of orientation) are always indicated as being north of Mari and in Harran, in the Temple of Sin. The Bible provides no information on the itinerary followed between Ur and Harran. Scholars think that the caravan went up the Euphrates, then up the Balikh. After indicating a stay of indeterminate length in Harran, the Bible says only that Terah died there, at the age of 205, and that Abraham was 75 when he took up the journey again with his family and his goods. This time the migration went from east to west, first as far as the Euphrates River, which they may have crossed at Carchemish, since it can be forded during low-water periods.

Here again, the Mari texts supply a reference, for they indicate that there were Benjaminites on the right bank of the river, in the lands of Yamhad (Aleppo), Qatanum (Qatna), and Amurru. Since the ancient trails seem to have been marked with sanctuaries, it is noteworthy that Nayrab, near Aleppo, was, like Harran and Ur, a center of the Sin cult and that south of Aleppo, on the road to Hamah, there is still a village that bears the name of Benjamin. The route is in the direction of the "land of Canaan," the goal of the journey.

If a stop in Damascus is assumed, the caravan must next have crossed the land of Bashan (the Hawran of today), first crossing the Jabboq, then the Jordan River at the ford of Damiya, and arriving in the heart of the Samaritan country, to reach at last the plain of Shechem, today Balatah, at the foot of the Gerizim and Ebal mountains. Shechem was at the time a political and religious centre, the importance of which has been perceived more clearly as a result of recent archaeological excavations. From the mid-13th to the mid-11th century Bc, Shechem was the site of the cult of the Canaanite god Ba'al-Berit (Lord of the Covenant). The architecture uncovered on the site by archaeologists would date to the 18th century Bc, in which the presence of the patriarchs in Shechem is placed.

The next stopping place was in Bethel, identified with present-day Baytin, north of Jerusalem. Bethel was also a holy city, whose cult was centered on El, the Canaanite god par excellence. Its name does not lend itself to confusion, for it proclaims that the city is the bet, "house," or temple, of El (God). The Canaanite sanctuary was taken over without hesitation by Abraham, who built an altar there and consecrated it to Yahweh, at least if the Yahwistic tradition in Genesis is to be believed.

Abraham had not yet come to the end of his journey. Between Shechem and Bethel he had gone about 31 miles. It was about as far again from Bethel to Hebron, or more precisely to the oaks of Mamre, "which are at Hebron" (according to the Genesis account). The location of Mamre has been the subject of some indecision. At the present time, there is general agreement in setting it 1.5 miles (3 km) northwest of Hebron at Ramat al-Khalil, an Arabic name which means the "Heights of the Friend," the friend (of God) being Abraham.

Mamre marked the site of Abraham's encampment, but this did not at all exclude episodic travels in the direction of the Negeb, to Gerar and Beersheba. Life was a function of the economic conditions of the moment, of pastures to follow and to find, and thus the patriarchs moved back and forth between the land of Canaan and the Nile River delta. They remained shepherds and never became cultivators.

It was in Mamre that Abraham received the revelation that his race would be perpetuated, and it was there that he learned that his nephew Lot had been taken captive. The latter is an enigmatic episode, an "erratic block" in a story in which nothing prepared the way for it. Suddenly, the life of the patriarch was inserted into a slice of history in which several important persons ("kings") intervene: Amraphel of Shinar, Arioch of Ellasar, Ched-or-laomer of Elam, and Tidal of Goiim. Scholars of previous generations tried to identify these names with important historical figures—e.g. Amraphel with Hammurabi of Babylon—but little remains today of these suppositions. The whole of chapter 14 of Genesis, in which this event is narrated, differs completely from what has preceded and what follows. It may be an extract from some historical annals, belonging to an unknown secular source, for the meeting of Melchizedek, king of Salem and priest of God Most High (El 'Elyon), and Abraham is impressive. The king-priest greets him with bread and wine on his victorious return and blesses him in the name of God Most High.

In this scene, the figure of the patriarch takes on a singular aspect. How is his religious behavior to be characterized? He swears by "the Lord God Most High"—i.e., by both Yahweh and El 'Elyon. It is known that, on the matter of the revelation of Yahweh to man, the biblical traditions differ. According to what scholars call the Yahwistic source (J) in the Pentateuch (the first five books of the Bible), Yahweh had been known and worshiped since Adam's time. According to the so-called Priestly source (P), the name of Yahweh was revealed only to Moses. It may be concluded that it was probably El whom the patriarchs, including Abraham, knew.

As noted before, in Mesopotamia the patriarchs worshiped "other gods." On Canaanite soil, they met the Canaanite supreme god, El, and adopted him, but only partially and nominally, bestowing upon him qualities destined to distinguish him and to assure his preeminence over all other gods. He was thus to become El 'Olam (God the Everlasting One),

El 'Elyon (God Most High), El Shaddai (God, the One of the Mountains), and El Ro'i (God of Vision). In short, the god of Abraham possessed duration, transcendence, power, and knowledge. This was not monotheism but monolatry (the worship of one among many gods), with the bases laid for a true universalism. He was a personal god too, with direct relations with the individual, but also a family god and certainly still a tribal god. Here truly was the "God of our fathers," who in the course of time was to become the "God of Abraham, Isaac, and Jacob.

It is not surprising that this bond of the flesh should still manifest itself when it came to gather together the great ancestors into the family burial chamber, the cave of Machpelah. This place is venerated today in Hebron, at the Haram al-Khalil (Holy Place of the Friend), under the mosque. Abraham, "the friend of God," was forevermore the depositary of the promise, the beneficiary of the Covenant, sealed not by the death of Isaac but by the sacrifice of the ram that was offered up in place of the child on Mount Moriah.

This "scholarly" review of the birth of monotheism sets the table for the alternative forms of monotheism that follow historically. Scholastically, the birth of monotheism and the Covenant has occurred though it is not marked with a historic moment other than the sacrifice of the ram in place of the child, Isaac.

Generally, some farmers in fertile areas were now able to produce more food than they and their household could consume. Even in the Bronze Age, there was the beginning of a division of labor such that some members of society produced tools and weapons, some specialized in building buildings and perhaps homes, and yet others were engaged in trading local commodities for goods produced elsewhere. Certainly, within the next thousand years or so some form of clergy had developed in some of the various forms of worship and belief. The basic idea to be addressed here is: Why did humanity evolve to belief, and how did belief continue to develop? Many have theorized on how or why belief developed. In his book, *Sapiens: A Brief History of Mankind,* Yuval Harari states,

> Religion has been the third great unifier of humankind, alongside money and empires. Since all social orders and hierarchies are imagined, they are fragile, and the larger the society, the more fragile it is. The crucial historical role of religion has been to give superhuman legitimacy to these fragile structures. Religions assert that our laws are not the result of human caprice but are ordained by an absolute and supreme authority.
>
> Further, he points out that in the hunter-gatherer era, religions were local since most foragers spent their whole lives in an area of no more than a thousand square miles. But the Agricultural Revolution seemed accompanied by a religious revolution that some associated with owning the animals and fields thus causing humanity to look to supernatural assistance in controlling the outcomes of fecundity and crop performance.

The Agricultural Revolution was not a singular event but rather a process occurring in different locations and at different times. The period, from around 8,000 BCE through something like the third century AD, did not mark an end to a focus on agricultural production but rather a shift in relative priority that occurs from time to time in the march of history. I have identified this shift in priority that occurred during the third century as the evangelizing of the world by monotheism from 300 AD until 1455 AD. This next period includes the zenith and downfall of the Roman Empire and most of the medieval period. The focus of this chapter is the prehistoric and early history Agricultural Revolution represented by the Stone Age, Bronze , and Iron Age during which the birth of Hinduism, Judaism, Jainism, Buddhism, Confucianism, and Christianity represent the breadth of faith and religious practice that came into humanity's practice.

Harari's hypothesis is that religion is one of three foundational myths enabling our current social structure. Personally, I find this a convenient argument frequently employed by secular materialists to replace human experience and historical events with a rationalization that fails to encompass the depth of human witness to religious beliefs. I would not deny that at some points people employed the supernatural as an explanation of observed phenomena that they possessed no applicable experience or knowledge to otherwise explain. A continuation of that observation is still with us today in the presentation of the God-of-the- gaps argument. Of course, this gap approach sets up a straw man exploited by the march of history that includes scientific discovery of physical rules or laws that explain and accurately predict cause and effect relationships between observed physical activity and resulting effect. Calvin, Augustine, and others have advised Christians to look to God's works in the cosmos as a way of understanding the awesome nature and scope of our God. So as science continues to unfold additional information about the physical nature of God's works, Christians continue to understand there are limits to the "laws of physics" that leave believers accepting God as the ultimate first cause, without whom there is no creation. Christians have the additional foundation to their belief in the life and example of Jesus and to a lesser degree, his disciples, apostles, and evangelists.

This period only covers the first three centuries of Christian belief when a few individuals recorded their witness of Jesus life and a few others wrote letters to the infant Church with expressions of instruction and initial theology. Constantine had not yet authorized Christianity in the Roman empire, Saint Jerome had not defined the Bible, and early Christians were persecuted by pagan religions and Judaism during this period and beyond. Druids practiced their rituals in Great Britton and portions of Gaul. Jews were primarily located in small communities in Israel. Christians were limited to small mostly underground churches around the eastern Mediterranean. The dominant religion in the west was the celebration of humanlike gods and goddesses each with their own domain or sphere of influence. Primary obedience was either to a local ruler of a local kingdom or to consolidated rule from Rome and its emperor. Leaders of pagan temples had influence over whatever government structure was in their area. The prevailing Roman Empire had practiced syncretization to the extent that the gods of Greece and other conquered lands had been absorbed into the pantheon of Roman gods. While there had to be some very sincere and deeply held beliefs on the part of some of the majority pagans of the period, history is replete with records of religion and religious leaders employing their position for political gain. Except for the Jews and the new upstart Christians, religion as historically portrayed seemed imbued with cynicism and self-interest. Yet humanity started wrestling with the perpetual question: Why are we here? This question is the basic consideration of faith and seems to be unapproachable by science. Science is principally involved with how did we get here and is there anyone else here or there?

In my opinion, the major contribution of this period to the history of mankind is the development of writing. This enabled an individual or group to pass their message or the record of the events they experienced, on to their successors.

Monotheistic Evangelism

~~~~

Man has settled down. He has planted crops and domesticated animals. Man is master of all he surveys, except himself and his fellow man. We are now about three hundred years after the birth of Christ. Many religions have been established, and Rome still has dominion over most of the known world. This period of transition will prevail through most of the Middle Ages until 1455 AD. There were several shaping events and people early in this period but, particularly when considering the development of faith, certainly a major figure was Constantine. Born in 283 AD, he was the son of Flavius Valerius Constantias, a military officer who in 293 was raised to the rank of Caesar or deputy emperor. His father's promotion left Constantine with his mother in the court of Diocletian in Turkey. In Turkey, he had to be aware of the severe persecution of Christians in the Eastern Empire. Constantias requested that his son join him around 305 AD, and together, they went to campaign in Britain where Constantias died in 306. Constantine had married a rival's daughter by 310 and thereafter invaded Italy where he defeated his rival and became emperor of the West. Constantine defeated the Eastern emperor in 324 and became sole emperor of the East and West of the Roman Empire.

The Battle of Milvian Bridge, when he became emperor of the West, was fought in 312 by Constantine in the name of the Christian God. In a series of letters extending from this time until the early 320s,

Constantine espoused his Christian theology including forgiveness of the Donatist priests and bishops and ultimately leading to his invitation to speak before the Council of Nicaea where the clergy was to address the issue of Arianism, the precise nature of the Trinity. Constantine dedicated Constantinople as the capital of the East and "a second Rome" in 330. From this period on, while Rome remained a wealthy, influential and even a religious capital, its political importance in the Roman Empire waned. During Constantine's later days, the Church of the Holy Sepulcher was discovered, and he instigated the building of a new basilica at the spot in addition to his support of several other churches throughout Italy and Turkey. The Roman Empire did not suddenly convert to Christianity under Constantine. It took centuries until Rome and then other areas of Europe became predominantly Christian.

Tradition, supported by isolated Christian communities in India and other locations in Asia, holds that when the apostles left Judea after some significant delay, Saint Thomas was dispatched to India. He was to have landed in Muziris (modern day North Paravur and Kodungalloor in Kerala state) in AD 52. However, there is no historical corroboration since the port was destroyed in 1341 by a flood. In any event, there is evidence of the spread of the gospel message east of Constantinople over the next four centuries. Some contend that the Christian church virtually exploded on the Indian continent as well as throughout Persia and on to China and even Japan. In his book, *The Lost History of Christianity: The Golden Age of the Church in the Middle East, Africa, and Asia*, Philip Jenkins explores the Christian church in the east and its ultimate shrinkage as Islam developed. Jenkins points out that:

By the fifth century, Christianity had five great patriarchates, and only one, Rome, was to be found in Europe. Of the others Alexandria stood on the African continent and three (Constantinople, Antioch and Jerusalem) were in Asia. After the fall of the Roman Empire in the West, Christianity maintained its cultural and intellectual traditions in the Eastern empire, in Asia Minor, Syria, and Egypt.

Around AD 300, Christianity was designated the official state religion in Armenia and remains so until today. Georgia followed shortly thereafter.

In his book, *Christianity: The First Three Thousand Years,* Darmaid MacCulloch spends considerable space in his historical review of the development of Christianity listing theologians and emperors who individually or in concert shaped the faith as it is observed today. Each of the twists and turns had significant impact on the theology or theologies that developed, and as a historian, he chronologically and geographically explains each impact. In this exposition, I will take an overly broad approach touching on what I perceive are the most significant points while encouraging any of my readers to spend the effort to wade through Mr. MacCulloch's 1,184 pages of detailed history to fully grasp the impact of each twist.

When Constantine declared that Constantinople was the second Rome, he apparently and indirectly encouraged a separate clerical evolution of a more Greek-based theology developing the Byzantine Catholic tradition. In retrospect, this seems to me a form of continuum of the earlier division among Christian followers of the Judean and Latin traditions. The Byzantine component of the Catholic church evangelized the majority of the Eastern Church and was differentiated, among other rites, by its positions on idolatry, married clergy, leavened bread in the Eucharist, strict use of Latin as the exclusive liturgical language, and obedience to the Bishop of Rome. It was the Byzantine church that, at one point, had a congregation of believers several times the followers of the Roman or Latin church.

While this evangelical conversion was progressing from Constantinople East, Paul and his successors turned west through Turkey to Rome. The steady growth of Christianity pushed back the prevailing polytheistic tradition succeeding from the empires of Greece and Rome in the West. Similarly, Hinduism was shifting to an exclusive presence on the Indian subcontinent. Buddhism and its affiliates spread through Asia along with Christianity. Early Christian missionaries, outside of the Byzantine tradition, assisted local governments as well as religious denominations with writing and diplomatic efforts.

As this expansion and growth of Christianity was taking place, a successful merchant in Mecca married a wealthy widow, Khadijah, and at age forty went to Mount Hira for meditation. These were the first steps in the revelation of Islam to Muhammad. This was AD 610 and by AD 632 all of the verses revealed to an illiterate Muhammad by Gabriel were compiled in the Qur'an. In the intervening period, Muhammad left Mecca under pressure of the ruling Quraish, a clan of polytheistic merchants and elders. The Prophet eventually ended up in Medina gathering converts along the way. By AD 630, Muhammad and his followers, now numbering in the tens of thousands, had captured Mecca without a battle and established it as the holy city of Islam. By the end of AD 633, Muhammad was dead, but his caliphate heritage lived on and expanded. Islam quickly replaced the animism and polytheism practiced by tribes in the Arab peninsula. Islam also replaced Byzantine Christianity and Zoroastrianism even though in this initial stage conversion was not required as Arabs gained control of the peninsula and began to reach out to Northern Africa. This period was known as the Umayyad period and its influence extended through the Iberian Peninsula. In AD 732 Charles Martel led his army of Franks and turned back the Umayyads, led by Rahman Al Ghafiqi, at the Battle of Tours and is credited with preserving Christianity in Europe. It was after this defeat that Islam shifted from a religion within the Arab culture pursuing an Arab empire to a Muslim empire that taxed or killed non-Muslims. This shift took place during the Abbasid period; however, large Christian populations remained in Syria and Egypt at least until the Mongol invasions of the thirteenth century. Baghdad was besieged in 1258, and the Mongols took over large areas of the Middle East. Over time, many of the Mongol conquerors were converted, many to Christianity while others converted to Islam. The success of the Mongols pushed the Turks into concentrated communities in Anatolia, and in turn, they pushed back driving the Mongols back through Asia and establishing the Ottoman Empire which continued until 1920.

As Islam and then the Mongols then Islam again raged back and forth through the Middle East and much of Asia, the monastic practitioners of Christianity found isolation to the north in Novgorod and eventually Muscovy. Over the next centuries, this northern branch of Eastern Christianity centered in what is now Russia and extended into Eastern Europe and the Balkans. This monastic-centered practice gave birth to the Orthodox denomination and generated divisions between Byzantine Catholics, Roman Catholics, and the Orthodox church. These differing interpretations of the same Bible eventually led to further differing denominations eventually including the family of Protestants.

As an aside, I find it personally hard to accept that reading of a selected portion of Holy Scripture can lead to a difference of faith sufficient to justify burning at the stake, going to war, shunning of one or ones who do not accept your interpretation or other forms of violent disagreement among God's chosen. The First Commandment identifies God as one who will not accept graven images and who is a jealous God. From that folktale of questionable origination in Exodus, a tale that was passed on orally for hundreds to thousands of years before being written, iconoclastic denominations such as Byzantine, Orthodox, and Amish develop theologies decrying statuary, paintings, and clothing fashions. I cannot accept a god of all creation being so petty as to take a human interpretation of a message inspired by God but written by foible humans and find one acceptable or unacceptable in His sight on such irrelevant rules.

While Christianity was expanding in the east and then was conquered and driven back into the Middle East, first Paul then other evangelists spread Christianity throughout the Roman Empire and then the successor Holy Roman Empire. In Europe, after the collapse of Rome, there were many city states with local rulers and independent armies occasionally in alliances. Charlemagne, a grandson of Charles Martel, was an exception, and he consolidated Europe under a strong Holy Roman Emperor during his reign. After his death, Europe again consisted of several smaller states through the balance of this medieval period. The primary international power in Eurasia during this period was the Roman Catholic church headquartered in the Holy See in Rome and overseen by the b ishop of Rome, the pope.

Sometime, around two thousand years before the birth of Jesus of Nazareth, humanity began to keep written records. Reading and writing were not widespread, but rather restricted to some rulers, clerics, and a group of scribes trained to create records on clay tablets or later papyrus. Later, centuries after the Crucifixion, the religions representing the majority of the world's population had been founded and humanity was able to establish a continuing culture of growth and improved productivity. The earth was still flat. There were limits as to how far a person could go before falling off the edge. God was directly responsible for many events that a yet to be developed science would later explain. Most of what happened to humanity was considered an act of supernatural cause. Local rulers were absolute in their realm and were almost universally supported by their local clergy. Merchants had a favored status since they produced revenue from other locations and had some ability to communicate with other cultures. Farmers and craftsmen had productive value. People without property ownership or skills had their choice of hard labor or the military. Faith was hope for the least, and religion was discipline maintaining status quo. Then things changed around 1455.

Literate Revolution

To this point, we have relied for our historical presentation primarily on the record of secular science or naturalism. The record includes:

- The origin of the planet 4.5 billion years ago.
- The evidence of single celled bacterial and archaeal cells almost four billion years ago.
- The introduction of eukaryotic cells about two billion years ago forming a base for multi celled life.
- The Columbian explosion of complex plant and animal life forms occurred about five hundred million years ago.
- Archeological evidence of *Homo erectus* around two million years ago and other humanoids from about three hundred fifty thousand years ago.
- *Homo sapiens* emerged about fifty thousand years ago and migrated throughout Africa, Europe, Asia, and even Australia and the Americas.
- During the period from the emergence of humans until approximately BCE 8000, humanity, as it was, existed in small bands of hunter-gatherers.
- About ten thousand years ago, there was archeological evidence that humanity began to gather in settlements that grew crops and herded domesticated animals.

- Ownership of animals and crops seemed to foster emphasis on supernatural forces perhaps to try and control and encourage success of agricultural activities.
- Four thousand five hundred years ago (2,500 BCE), humanity started to record crop sizes and inventories, trading transactions, legal proceedings, rituals and hymns, and some narrative writing, including poetry.
- Hinduism, a polytheistic and, by some accounts, animistic religion, was evident north of the Indian subcontinent.
- Persia (550 BCE) then Greece (400 BCE) and then Rome (146 BCE), all polytheistic cultures dominated the known western world,
- Abraham, Moses, Jesus and Muhammad, all monotheists, had lived and their evangelists, including Thomas and Paul had spread their word by persuasion and sometimes conquest.
- The Bible was organized by Saint Jerome from several different sources and translated to Latin.
- Muhammad's daughter and son-in-law Ali had published the handwritten Qur'an.
- Nation states had been born in Europe, and while changes would continue to occur, nations with established national borders would, from time to time, attempt to extend their influence and claims beyond their borders.

By the fifteenth century AD, population had increased severalfold and was well into the millions of human inhabitants. Still, books were rare and very expensive. News was spread by word of mouth to the general populations and by courier and scribes among the rulers and elite. Reviewing the above list, not only had the epochal events within the list occurred, but the time between civilization changing watermarks had compressed significantly from millions of years to hundreds of thousands of years to hundreds of years.

Another epochal event occurred in 1455 when one hundred eighty copies of the forty-two-line Bible were distributed in accord with purchase agreements negotiated by Johannes Gutenberg with various dioceses around Europe. This is the first time that printing presses with moveable type were employed to mass produce, relatively inexpensively, a volume of books. This was, if not the birth of the reformation, certainly its formative infancy as well as an extension of the Renaissance which had begun earlier in Italy. It was the beginning of literacy being within the reach and an advantage to the common man. Over a short period of time, books were published in volume, and the Bible became a household item in native tongue rather than a priceless relic available only to the clergy.

In the interest of full disclosure, my middle name is Schaefer, the family name of my mother, which dates to origins in Germany and includes one Peter Schaeffer, Gutenberg's apprentice and son-in-law to Johannes Fust. It was Fust who financed Gutenberg's printing shop and eventually took him into bankruptcy. After the bankruptcy, Fust and Schaeffer opened the first publishing house employing moveable-type printing presses.

Now the genie was out of the bottle. The man on the street found value in being able to read and interpret all published or private information available in writing or printed text. Within generations, education was expanded because it could be leveraged into insight for the ambitious. One could read the Bible. It did not require rote memorization or a handed down quotation from the clergy or one of their minions. While in some denominations of monotheistic religions, the clergy still controlled the official interpretation of Holy Text, the words of the text were now available to the laity who, in some cases, challenged clerical interpretation.

We are dealing with the period from 1455 until 1776. Reading and education grew in influence, the New World was discovered; the Age of Enlightenment was born. Politics became subject to a social compact, and Newton discovered gravity. In the prior period, Jesus's ministry surpassed the law with love. Saint Paul democratized the faith by preaching to the gentiles. Yet, during Christianity's first great evangelical period, because literacy was limited, religion and the Latin tradition of the Christian religion particularly remained a top-down practice from clergy and ruler to congregant. Kings and occasionally queens ruled by divine right, and sometimes, it was hard to distinguish whether guidance on morality, ritual, good citizenship, and daily living came from the priest or the local agent of your ruling government. Then each diocese and eventually each home had its own copy of the Bible, and the common man was encouraged to read the scriptures, even in their own tongue.

In reading of this continuous shifting and adjusting of faith as an historic process, I saw a pattern develop that I believe continues into our present world. Selected readings from Holy Scripture—Bible, Qur'an, or Old Testament—took on special significance to a sect, diocese, or denomination of believers and revised interpretation was declared and faith re-formed to adopt new emphasis. Prehistoric modifications from animism to polytheism were not recorded for subsequent analysis since writing was not known, and modification seemed more a simple matter of who prevailed in battle. When Christianity began, upon the occasion of the resurrection, and shortly after the death of the first martyr, Saint Stephen, as one of the Sanhedrin that condemned him converted on the road to Damascus, Paul started preaching to the Latin Gentiles. Employing differing theology, Peter, John, and the disciples other than Timothy stayed more attached to Judea and the Jewish and Greek cultures. It required two meetings among the early evangelists to encourage the Church Universal open to all who believed.

A few hundred years later, Constantine I seemed to reopen some residual elements of the Latin Greek division. He declared Constantinople the second Rome, and over time, the separation widened into the Byzantine Catholic, Roman Catholic division. Among components of the division, the Byzantine Church looked upon religious Roman art and sculpture as idolatry, did not emphasize transubstantiation, did not require unleavened host, and did not require wine as elements of the Eucharist. Further, married men could become priests and were not required to pledge obedience to the Bishop of Rome. These differences resulting in two divisions of the "One Church" continued even as challenges from Islam grew from the seventh century AD into the Middle Ages.

In the late fifteenth century, Girolamo Savonarola, a Dominican Priest of Florence, started interpreting Roman theology to include renunciation of Medici corruption and Medici support for artistic beauty. With invasion pressure from France mounting, he developed a new republican structure, and while not a member of the government, his sermons shaped the idea that governments were to represent the governed and promote God's kingdom on earth. Pope Alexander VI, a Borgia, offered Fr. Savonarola a cardinal's cap, but he refused, and shortly thereafter, the reformer was imprisoned, tortured, and killed. His reformer's zeal was picked up by another priest born in 1469 in Rotterdam. Desiderius Erasmus and his brother were educated in monastic institutions, and Desiderius became proficient in languages and developed as a humanist theologian working to reform the Roman Church, particularly taking aim at indulgences and the scripturally unsupported concept of a purgatory where the recently passed could realize improved conditions from purchases by their surviving family members. Erasmus used satirical humor as one of his weapons and no doubt that made some of his barbs more tolerable. He completed his re-translation of Jerome's Vulgate in 1516 where he corrected the text in one area from *do penance* to *show repentance*, a potentially significant change in religious ritual.

Erasmus stayed within the church. The next reformer priest was a monastic in Witten, Germany, and building on the humanist tradition of reform, Martin Luther took exception to the selling of indulgences, but while questioning the possible idolatry of religious art, he developed a more tolerant position that such art was for "recognition, for witness, for commemoration and for a sign. " After meetings with Cajetan, a papal envoy, disagreement hardened into dispute and in 1520 excommunication. The Diet of Worms was convened in 1521, and Luther was directed to observe obedience. Luther responded that he, "would not obey a monstrous godlessness." During Luther's theological development, the Schaefer-Fust publishing company saw several similar organizations develop across Europe, rapidly expanding the availability of the printed word.

A next step in the Christian schism was encouraged by a pastor in Zurich, Switzerland—Huldrych Zwingli. Pastor Zwingli sympathized with the Byzantine theory of art and music as idolatry and improper in church. Further, the Eucharist represented to him "something humanity did for God not what God did for humanity," a sharp departure from Rome's interpretation. Similarly, baptism was the community welcoming a child, not a washing away of sin. It was in 1529 at the Diet of Speyer that the term Protestant was coined. The positions of Luther and Zwingli represented clerical reform supported by "magisterial power." This practice continued as the Anabaptists came on the scene. They could find no direct biblical requirement for the practice of infant baptism. They had a distrust of the church's alliance with imperial power such as Constantine and the use of councils, such as Nicaea. Throughout northern and central Europe—Germany and Scandinavia—local inspiration and local denominations became a general observation. In the East in 1526, the Turks defeated the Habsburgs, so while France and the remnants of Austria, Italy, and the Iberian Peninsula remained Roman Catholic, the power of the Pope was radically diminished.

Now William Tyndale (1494– 1536) came into prominence in England. He was raised in the western borderlands where he developed an ear for language including Welsh and an appreciation that the rhythms and narrative force of English might afford a better translation vehicle for the Old Testament than Greek or Latin. Tyndale followed in the tradition established by John Wycliffe (1320–1384) an Oxford scholar who was involved in Biblical studies when the Black Plague devastated Europe from 1348–1350. The apparent powerlessness of the Church to provide protection from this terror that decimated up to 30 percent of the then current population led Wycliffe to disclose in a native tongue, English, what the Latin Vulgate Bible said so average people could examine what God's word actually advised. As a master at Oxford, he used his skills and was assisted by other academics and students, producing the first edition in 1384 with subsequent editions in 1388 and 1395. The Wycliffe Bible was hand published and some have estimated that only two hundred fifty copies were ever published. The prevailing Roman Catholic Church opposed the publication and eventually declared Wycliffe a heretic. Many regard this publication as the birth of the reformation. Keep in mind that Erasmus published his translation in a new version of the vulgate in Latin in 1516, and

Luther faced the Diet of Worms in 1521 and magisterial support for an independent diocese was weakening the power of the papacy. This is when the Tyndale Bible was published in England where Henry VIII was fighting with the pope about annulling his first marriage. With support from Thomas Cromwell as prime minister and Thomas Cranmer as archbishop up to two thousand six hundred copies of the Tyndale Bible were distributed to each diocese in England. Even this self-centered establishment of a new church to justify a divorce was traced back to a literate act of revelation and reform. Of course, about two hundred fifty years later, the church established as a result of Henry's hubris; it experienced many alterations and adjustments as the upstart colonies in America fought and won a revolution for religious and political independence.

The evolution of faith as an interpretation of the revealed word of God or Allah went through many changes during this three-hundred-twenty-year period. Islam continued its expansion into southeast Asia and schisms developed within the Shia and Sunni denominations as well as differences in emphasis among different imams and national congregations. The reformation of Christianity, initiated by Luther's thesis in 1517, continued through to the colonization of America and gave rise eventually to a political doctrine of separation of church and state as well as the theological presentation of the concept of the priesthood of man. A common thread in all religions seems to have been greater diversity in relationship among the clergy, congregation, and God or Allah. Roman Catholic practices were modified to stop the sale of indulgences, and in 1540, Pope Paul III commissioned the Jesuits who became the "soldiers of Christ" counteracting the spread first of Islam and then Protestantism.

There is no question that during this period, in particular, with the initial emphasis on things intellectual, religious activity, and government did intertwine and governments utilized religion to legitimize their existence and policies. However, it is also well observed that with the ability to write and disseminate ideas with facility, religious thought gained depth and critical analysis.

Beginnings of
Democracy

The Age of Enlightenment, personified by Locke, Rousseau, Descartes, Voltaire, Hume, Smith, and Kant is sometimes credited with starting around 1620 but was surely in full bloom by 1789, the year of the beginning of the French Revolution. The year 1776 marked the beginning of the American Revolution which culminated in ratification of our Constitution in 1788. The USA, even up to 1865 and the end of the Civil War, remained a predominantly agrarian society. While the Constitution guaranteed freedom to worship in any faith tradition an individual selected or developed, we were openly a Christian, God-fearing society. It was in the United States where the various forms of reformation Protestantism, initially developed by European theologians, took root. While the Roman Catholic church prospered and grew in the USA, it wasn't until 1928 that the first Catholic Presidential candidate was nominated. Al Smith lost handily to Herbert Hoover. No Catholic ran for President again until 1962 when John Kennedy was not only nominated but also won the presidency. Issues with the Mormons, Scientology, and Islam were not yet even in view.

In an article written for the Smithsonian magazine, Kenneth C. Davis, an author of twelve or so books primarily on American history, made several observations on the history and tradition of religious freedom in America. His review illustrated an uneven series of events that grew the USA into the paragon of religious liberty it is today. For example, French Huguenots, Calvinist Protestants, established a colony in 1564 at Fort Caroline near Jacksonville, Florida. The Spanish had established a colony at St. Augustine and Pedro Menendez de Aviles by 1565, the Spanish commander, subsequently sent a letter to King Philip II stating that he had "hanged all those we had found in Fort Caroline because they were scattering the odious Lutheran doctrine in these provinces." Virginia tended to be an Anglican stronghold; New England was the province of Puritans where four Quakers were hanged in Boston for persistently returning to the city to profess their beliefs. Maryland had a majority Roman Catholic population that barred Jews from public office and the other states in the colonies each had their own denominational religious support or restrictions. Ultimately it was James Madison, before his efforts to father the Constitution, who authored an essay, "Memorial and Remonstrance Against Religious Assessments" which laid out reasons why the state had no business supporting religious instruction and later by extension any particular religion. This essay started a drumbeat picked up by Jefferson, Washington, and Franklin among others that led to our secular government reflecting the sentiment expressed by Madison late in his life that "I have no doubt… that religion and government will both exist in greater purity, the less they are mixed together."

While Europe and the Middle East developed nation states and rulers each bound to a state religion, the USA placed independence at the apex of its list of priorities. Protestantism and American independence are very compatible ideologically. They both elevate the role and contribution of the individual; both emphasize the separate roles of government and religion, and both look to an egalitarian treatment of all citizens regardless of rank or occupation. No doubt the character of the frontier America, where early settlers were challenged by nature and native Americans who saw their territory being invaded, led individuals to fend for themselves in all facets of life, including religion. Until the latter half of the nineteenth century, there were a few cities, some towns, and many independent farms scattered over a vast countryside. In the more populous northern half of the country, the climate dictated that a farmer plant as early in the spring as possible, hope for rain in the summer, and harvest in the fall before winter storms drove people inside to get ready for next year. The Southeast developed a modification of this sequence. The growing season was longer providing for a different variety of crops. While God or Mother Nature still ruled crop yields, seasonal swings were not of as great a magnitude. With extended labor, larger farm units could be developed providing larger crops such as cotton, and further north tobacco, for sale to either local or foreign markets. Labor was required on northern farms, but each unit was smaller, and crops of grains, vegetables, and livestock were not as readily impacted by adding a large labor force per unit on a permanent basis with attendant involvement in housing and oversight. In the Southeast, however, slavery made the economy expand and made life quite comfortable for the successful plantation owner.

In smaller settlements in the north and Midwest, artisans forged horseshoes, coopered barrels, fired porcelain and china, created weapons and ammunition, and offered clothing imported from England and tailored locally. Down south, the plantation had its own artisans, generally talented slaves for local needs, and other goods were secured during periodic trips to port cities where crops were sold for export either to the north or to Europe. Other goods such as weaponry and clothing were purchased from importers. As in all generalizations, not every southerner was a sophisticated plantation owner and not every northerner was an unsophisticated dirt farmer. But there was a common denominator in the great majority of cases during the eighteenth and nineteenth centuries in America, all Christian homes outside of the few major population centers in New York, Boston, Savannah, and Philadelphia had their own personal Bible, and it was generally well thumbed. Both the Roman and Anglican church of the era stressed apostolic succession and more formal liturgies. The reformed churches growing out of the Diet of Worms and succeeding theological events, while having differences among the Lutherans, Baptists, Methodists, and Presbyterians for example, all stressed the priesthood of man which fit the culture of agricultural frontier America where many congregations saw their circuit riding preacher three or four times a year. Individualism was valued in pre-Civil War America both in the culture and in religion.

However, while England had established her dominance in textile manufacturing and other new machines of production, that reality was challenged by a growing manufacturing capability in the northern USA. The seeds of the Industrial Revolution, planted in Europe, took root and grew to a bumper crop in the USA where industrial production and a larger more concentrated population were to be the deciding factors in the Civil War while it lasted from 1862 through 1865. Slavery ended and that threatened southern society. While farmers still dominated the economic health of the North for years after the war, the influence of manufacturing and "metropolitanization" started a continuing road to dominance on society with concomitant influence on religion in America and over time the form, content and practice of faith.

INDUSTRIAL REVOLUTION
1865–1945

A Scotsman named James Watt, in 1787, unveiled his patented improvement on the Newcomen steam engine and initiated the Industrial Revolution. For the first time , man could now convert heat power to mechanical power anywhere he could find or transport fuel such as wood or coal and add a supply of water to convert heat energy into mechanical energy powering pumps, weaving machines, and other manufacturing devices. Great Britain started the yet continuing march toward ever improving manufacturing productivity through expanding mechanization and automation. While some of the impact of Mr. Watt's invention started to find its way to New England after 1800, it wasn't until the Civil War that major impetus was felt, speeding the advantage of steam power for manufacturing, rail and water transport.

In the interest of full disclosure again, I have in my possession a diary of my g randfather while on a trip to England, the Isle of Man and Paris in 1888. My great-grandfather was a builder of wooden ships that plied the Great Lakes and was facing the necessity to convert to steam powered iron vessels. William H. Radcliffe migrated to the USA somewhere around 1855 when he was thirty years old. When he was thirty-two, he married my great-grandmother in Cleveland, Ohio. He and my grandfather sailed, in salon class, to England on the Umbria of the Cunard Line, an iron ship with a steam engine.

When not visiting family on the Isle of Man or in Liverpool, they spent much of their time visiting dry-docks and shipyards.

As I looked back from this period, the Industrial Revolution to the Stone Age, I posit that humanity's progression from its roots in Africa through today is a progression in search of readily available energy. Humanity had the use of fire to keep warm and defend itself from other predators even in the Stone Age. This conversion from fuel to heat was initially restricted to wood which was more readily available than it is today. Jared Diamond in *Guns, Germs, and Steel* theorized that western culture became dominant because initially western Europe and then the USA represented more fertile paths of immigration, seeking agricultural productivity until it became the dominant habit. His argument is well drawn and has merit, but I believe that at a greater depth, energy was the driver. Until the Industrial Revolution, wood was the dominant resource. To be sure, iron was of great value as was the coal to purify the ore into a metal for shaping, but wood fueled many fires, shaped ships, and created spars to catch the wind. While there were still forests in Europe, wood was becoming scarcer in some regions. Those returning from early trips to the New World, be they Norse, Spanish, French, or British, remarked about the lush landscape and readily available supply of wood for building, heating, and mending spars. Then came Watt's steam engine, and coal became king. Initially, coal was the fuel for Roman baths back in the second century, but there was a gap in coal's historical development from AD 410, when the Romans left Briton, until the twelfth century when carbon strata were exposed on some parts of the seashore and used for smelting, lime burning, and metal working. Usage grew even though this sea-coal was not suitable for home heating. Sir George Bruce opened the first mine, in 1575, to extract coal, and with improvement in hearth design, it began to be used to heat homes. Recognize that as the value of coal increased, Great Britain's influence on the world stage increased. It has been stated that by 1700, Britain produced about three million long tons per year, by 1780 that figure grew to 6.25 long tons, then by 1815 reached sixteen million tons, and finally, 1830 over thirty million tons.

Other factors were also taking place affecting industrialization, generally, and USA industrialization, specifically. By the mid-eighteenth century, the British colonies had become the most prosperous, but the exodus of skilled labor from England became a matter for parliament to debate, calling for a total ban on emigration to the colonies. However, independence and continuing harassment of shipping and transportation in the sea lanes slowed immigration to the USA. The first census was taken in the US in 1790, and it totaled three million, nine hundred thousand people, nearly twenty percent of whom were African Americans. Native Americans were not counted. Immigration had slowed, and until peace with England was reestablished in 1814, it ran around six thousand people a year. Then New York, Philadelphia, Boston, and Charleston were overwhelmed with newcomers, many sick or dying from the long slow journey. The Steerage Act of 1819 was quickly passed requiring ship captains to keep passenger records and provide humane conditions for those on board. There were several other factors in the period from 1790 to 1865 affecting immigration and industrialization:

- The Napoleonic wars 1803–1815 created turmoil throughout Europe conscripting youth and tying down their elders.
- The Irish potato famine 1840–1850 starving approximately 1.5 million in Ireland and sending a like number to the US during this period.
- The California Gold Rush 1848–1855.
- The Franco-Prussian War 1870.
- The US Civil War 1861–1865.

Each of these events had their own unique impact. The Franco-Prussian War brought many Germans to the Midwest, either to avoid the war or after the peace. The Gold Rush and the railroad expansion brought many Asians, particularly Chinese to the West Coast. The Potato famine brought Irish and strong Roman Catholic communities reaching from Boston even into Wisconsin. Between 1880 and 1930 over twenty-seven million people entered the United States.

With this influx of new labor, a ready supply of iron, coal and water, and a large undeveloped land mass, the USA became the world's laboratory for industrialization, urbanization, and entrepreneurship. As an example of the appeal of this new land of opportunity it was estimated that in the 1880s alone, up to 9 percent of the entire population of Norway emigrated to America. This amalgam of longtime colonialists, African Americans just freed from slavery, newly independent Roman Catholic Irish, persecuted European masses, and some mix of artisans and academics impacted the culture in which American faith was forged.

There is no theology of American Christianity. There is just Christianity. But to deny that this unique mix of cultures in a period of rapid economic and technological change did not impact religious thought and practice in America and eventually throughout the world is to fly in the face of observable fact. In a portion of this period from 1835 to 1900 alone:

- the electric relay was developed (1835),
- telegraph and Morse code developed, (1837),
- the first transatlantic telegraph cable was laid (1858),
- the first transcontinental railroad was completed (1869),
- Maxwell's Treatise on Electricity and Magnetism was published (1873),
- Edison invented the phonograph (1877),
- the first functional light bulb was introduced (1879),
- the rabies vaccine was developed by Pasteur (1885),
- Karl Benz sold the first commercial automobile (1886),
- Aspirin was patented (1889),
- and the USA gained control of Cuba, Puerto Rico, and the Philippines after the Spanish American War (1898).
- This is certainly not a complete list of world-shaping events in this sixty-five-year period but is indicative of the beginning of the acceleration brought on in the early period of scientific and technological advance. The turn of the century brought on Max Planck, Albert Einstein, Niels Bohr, and Werner Heisenberg. Quantum physics and the

birth of atomic fusion were just around the corner. The early 1900s also saw man's first flight in a heavier than air craft, the opening of Ransom E. Olds's automobile plant in Detroit followed by the birth of General Motors in 1908, and Henry Ford's development of the first moving assembly line in 1913. Man was mobile on earth, sea, and sky. If the second half of the 1800s was the time of steam transportation and wired communication, the first half of the 1900s became the time of the internal combustion engine, radio, and the birth of Hollywood and eventually that new medium, television. The period from 1900 to 1945 saw two world wars. In the period from 1880 to 1930 America greeted over twenty-seven million new residents. Of course, in 1929 the Great Depression began and carried into the early 1930s.

Reflecting on the events from the end of the Civil War until almost the end of World War II is a dizzying experience. First light, first flight, first and second worldwide fights. This series affected the individual cultures of all countries, some more severely than others, but none escaped the destructive impact of war, world economic failure, technologic advances, widespread epidemic, or the challenges to optimism and faith these events engendered. It might be that upstart America was the most naïve society entering this period and one of the more cynical by the end of the period, but from what I have read and indirectly observed of my preceding generations (parents and grandparents etc.), we were not that unique in the world regarding our opinions of world events and our reactions to them. That reaction was not universal or uniform but rather took several different courses:

- Evangelical Christians followed popular preachers in significant numbers, including figures like Billy Sunday, Harry Ironside (Moody Church), Aimee Semple McPherson, Karl Barth, Jerry Falwell, Timothy J. Keller, and Billy Graham.

- Television became the major entertainment and news medium as well as bringing forth television ministries including Bishop Fulton J. Sheen, Robert Schuller, Jimmy Swaggart, John Osteen, Pat Robertson, Rex Humbard, Jim and Tammy Faye Bakker, and Reverend Ike. Millions of people followed this more fundamental and generally conservative brand of American Christianity, though there were preachers of similar threads of theology spread around the world.
- Science emphasized secular materialism and neo-Darwinian evolution as the only acceptable doctrines of the truly educated practitioner worthy of grant funding, particularly federal grant funding.
- Traditional mainline denominations and dioceses started to lose congregants.
- There was, from time to time, some emphasis on newer non-traditional practices of faith including Christian Science, Scientology, and Mormonism.
- In his book, *Theology of the Old Testament*, Walter Brueggemann discusses the challenges facing any scriptural translation and interpretation, which includes contextual consideration both in the period when it was written and contemporaneous context for scripture interpretation. I am reading Justice Stephan Breyer's book, *The Court and the World*, and one of his major points of discussion revolves around the characteristic observed in case histories, that interpretation of existing law changes as a consequence of changing conditions in the world. Look again at the review of some of the significant events listed above that occurred in an eighty-year period from 1865 until 1945, and it seems evident that maintaining a Christian faith based upon a supernatural being who listens to each of us individually would face new challenges to its credibility. It is likely that the atheistic argument would have support from many basically innocent individuals who experienced loss of security, loss of fortune or loss of life because of

technology acceleration, occurrence of world conflicts as well as worldwide economic depression and epidemic. End of days theology, theology that embraced science either directly or in title identification and fundamentalist focus on literal Biblical interpretation gained traction and, in some cases, embraced denial.

ATOMIC AGE 1945–2000

The United States dropped the world's first atomic bomb on Hiroshima, Japan on August 6,1945. Three days later, August 9, 1945, Nagasaki, Japan was the target. An estimated total of approximately one hundred twenty-nine thousand to two hundred thousand Japanese people were killed. The USA Chief of Staff, supported by allied estimates, had projected that the softening blanket bombing as well as artillery barrages and ultimately house to house fighting as part of an allied invasion would produce deaths exceeding one million, including hundreds of thousands of Allied Powers's troops, a majority of whom would be Americans. While some nuclear weapon development was occurring outside of the USA, America was the solitary possessor of nuclear weapons at the dawning of the Atomic Age.

Harry Truman had succeeded FDR as President and was surprisingly re-elected in 1948. By the time General Eisenhower became President in 1953, Russia had tested its first nuclear weapon in 1949. Russia and China signed an agreement in 1951, whereby China was to supply uranium ore in exchange for technical assistance in developing their own nuclear weapon. The United Kingdom tested a plutonium weapon in October 1952. The United States tested the first nuclear fusion bomb, the H-Bomb in November 1952. The Soviet Union followed with its first H-bomb test in August 1953. USA and the United Kingdom inked a Mutual Defense Agreement in 1958 after the UK had tested an H-bomb. In February of 1960, France joined the list of nations with a demonstrated nuclear weapon.

Over time Pakistan, India, and Israel also had tested nuclear fusion devices. In 2006, North Korea tested its first nuclear weapon in 2006 and in 2016, North Korea tested a fusion device. The Nuclear Non-proliferation Treaty was opened for signatures in July 1968, and presently, there are one hundred sixty-nine signatories. Non-participating states include India, Israel, Pakistan, and North Korea.

Bombs are not the exclusive application of nuclear fission. It was proposed in 1940 that this exothermic reaction could be designed to produce steam and thus propulsion and electric power. President Eisenhower announced the Atoms for Peace program in 1953 to identify and exploit the newly developed controlled fission reaction. The world's first nuclear powered electricity generator was put online in Obninsk, Russia, in 1953, located approximately a hundred kilometers southwest of Moscow. The USA focused on developing a Pressurized Water Reactor (PWR), and this approach resulted in the launch of the USS Nautilus in 1954 with surface vessels to follow in 1959. The first commercial power plant, Yankee River was completed by Westinghouse in 1960. General Electric commissioned a Boiling Water Reactor (BWR) at Dresden in 1960. Power plants went through several generations of design improvement as well as periods of rapid development and pullbacks in construction of new facilities. The generation of 16 to 17 percent of total power demand has been a more or less steady level of capacity supplied by nuclear generating facilities since the 1970s.

We have nuclear weapons and nuclear power, a trade off? Not quite. Three Mile Island, Chernobyl, and Fukushima argue the distaff side of peaceful use of atomic energy, at least for power generation. March 28, 1979, was the date of the worst US disaster at Three Mile Island Unit 2 near Middletown, Pennsylvania. The plant went on line in February 1978 and Babcock and Wilcox supplied the reactor control system. This was a period preceding highly integrated microchip computer systems with high-speed reliable configurations with built in redundancies. While computers were regularly applied as supervisory devices to optimize production, a combination of conventional instrumentation and single loop analog controllers exercised most direct control. At Three Mile Island, there apparently was a buildup of some mineral deposit on a valve that plant engineers tried to dislodge. In attempting this backflush, the valve remained open unbeknownst to the operators. Before this error was discovered, heat had started to buildup and eventually errors and design flaws combined to start a reactor meltdown. Single loop control failed to recognize the problem when the position detector on the valve failed. More modern plants use computer generated heat balances to detect heat buildup sooner. Fortunately, before things got completely out of control, the situation was recognized, and plant operators were able to stabilize the reactor without major release of radioactive gas, water, or particulate. The unit was retired from service, decommissioned, and decontaminated. Unit 1 was relicensed to continue in operation until 2034, at which time it is anticipated that both units will be decommissioned, decontaminated, and torn down.

Chernobyl was a different story. Design engineers, apparently relatively newly minted, wanted to run some experiments on how long power remained available when generators were shut down. The engineers ran the plant in a manner beyond design limits and over the objection of the plant operators. In this situation, the reactor shield was dislodged by a serious explosion during a meltdown and radioactive steam and particulate escaped into the atmosphere. One person died as a result of the explosion; one more died the next day as a result of Acute Radiation Syndrome (ARS). Shortly thereafter an additional twenty-eight persons died of ARS, primarily plant operators and first responders. There is a statistically unusual quantity of childhood thyroid cancers in the region, but this has not been directly attributed to the meltdown. In this case, there were direct casualties, the reactor was encased in a concrete sarcophagus pumped down from helicopters and the surrounding area was evacuated. Some time ago there was a PBS special on the benefit to nature of depopulating the area and leaving it open to wildlife such as caribou and wolves. The area is now open for tourist tours where exposure can be monitored and kept to an acceptable level.

Fukushima is yet a different set of circumstances. The Fukushima power plant included six BWR reactors originally designed by General Electric. The accident was initiated primarily by the tsunami following the Tōhoku earthquake on March 11, 2011. Immediately after the earthquake, the active reactors automatically shut down their sustained fission reactions. However, the tsunami disabled the emergency generators that would have provided power to control and operate the pumps necessary to cool the reactors. The insufficient cooling led to three nuclear meltdowns, hydrogen-air explosions, and the release of radioactive material in Units 1, 2, and 3 from March 12 to March 15. Loss of cooling also caused the pool for storing spent fuel from Reactor 4 to overheat on March 15 due to the decay heat from the fuel rods. Approximately one hundred twenty thousand people have been dislocated from an area of 20 kilometers surrounding the plant. Over eighteen thousand five hundred people died as a result of the earthquake and consequent tsunami, but no deaths were directly attributed to the nuclear meltdown.

There have been three power plant incidents in the fifty-seven years since the first commercial plant went on line in 1960. As far as I am aware, there has been one US and one Russian naval accident among the thousands of surface and undersea nuclear-powered vessels. Statistically, these numbers may seem acceptable, except for the duration of the effects and the aftermath. We are not regularly informed of the consequences of military incidents. We know Chernobyl and Fukushima have left scars of lives lost, lives threatened, and physical property left fallow by contamination. This is where the Atomic Age meets faith. Atomic weapons yield destruction of immense proportions capable of destroying hundreds of thousands to millions of lives per use, and there are inventories of thousands of potential uses armed and ready. Atomic power can accidentally kill innocents near generation facilities and render vast areas of real estate unusable for generations. The atom has impact beyond any force or army previously known to mankind. On our own, we can destroy significant chunks of God's creation and perhaps the majority of humankind. How does God's Old Testament covenant or New Testament promise of Jesus have relevance?

It is my recollection that in the late '60s or early '70s, Time magazine issued one of their regular weekly publications with a cover in black upon which appeared in white font the words, "God is Dead?"

That was a challenge to faith at that point in time, and it continued with emphasis for some period, only diminishing as the world continued to survive under the regime of MAD—Mutually Assured Destruction. Secular materialism, sharing opinion and publication space with scientific atheism, ruled the day and dominated academe. If you were looking for a research grant for scientific work, it did not hurt your chances if you underscored your support for neo-Darwinian evolution and sub-atomic random accidents of a chaotic cosmos as the driving force behind our accidental presence. Talk of a design or a purpose was, and in many quarters still is, considered naïve and adolescent at best. Church attendance, particularly in main line protestant churches began a decline that continues unto today. The challenges to a healthy and sincere faith came from several quarters:

- Scientifically, many phenomena considered within the domain of the supernatural became identified and defined within the realm of scientific predictability and repeatability;
- Politically and geographically, the chasm between the secular and the believing communities widened and deepened;
- Within the "churched" community, there appeared sharper differences between traditional and contemporary religious observance;
- The pace of contemporary life seems incompatible with periods of quiet contemplation which have traditionally supported religious faith;
- Social conscience seems less individual choice and sacrifice and more governmental program or institutional charity;
- Driven by advertising, particularly on the growing medium of television, the United States, followed by the rest of the developed world, adopted "consumerism" as its economic driver, and things became the symbols of success and promised immediate gratification, satisfaction, and fulfilment.

But there seems to always be a dialectical reality in effect as well. Biblically, this reality is stated in 1 Corinthians Chapter 15 verse 21 : "For since by man came death, by man came also the resurrection of the dead." This theme was used by Handel in his messiah as well. The unity of diametric opposites is demonstrated by our world in many observed phenomena within our existence. This dialectic is once again demonstrated by the increase in non-denominational evangelism bringing about increases in mega-churches and contemporary worship services, illustrating a strong need for faith supported by the reaction of the faith seekers to the same circumstances challenging traditional believers.

The continuing need for faith as a resource to assist humanity in coping with the challenges of existence is not a terminal phenomenon. Without faith in a purpose to life, behaviors necessary for a quality of life can still be observed. B ut a reliance on kindness, moderation, self-sacrifice, love, and wisdom as random occurrences propelled by DNA and chemicals would seem to leave society very vulnerable, as compared to the possibility of existence for the benefit of others being a valid religious mantra generally, though not constantly, observed. Without a belief in God or a supernaturally driven purpose to our existence, we can still live and behave in socially acceptable ways because we have laws and customs as well as social pressure, tradition, and history that influence us collectively and individually. We can still want to do "the right thing" and respect our neighbor. With faith, there is an ever-present motivation to satisfy self, others, and God with our continuing attempt to live productive lives serving others. Yes, that motivation can be and has been perverted from time to time, but hopefully, faith supported by and enabled with increasing knowledge of the material wonders of science will not again allow religious belief to be an instrument of evil forces.

Information Age 2000–

I have elected to start the information age with January 1, 2000, the beginning of a new millennium. Remember the real sense of panic generated by the computer industry and its user community, practically every commercial entity then. There was concern for payroll processing, accounts receivable posting, and other critical commercial applications that typically employed the date format as mm/dd/yy, where the year kept increasing, such as '98, '99, '00, oops. We suddenly became very aware that our day-to-day living was impacted by our information handling systems and a legion of programmers.

Since that time, we have embraced iPad, iWatch, on board GPS, on board auto fuel monitoring and computer control, laptop, tablet, voice recognition, an expanded internet, and a connected society of big data, hacking and identity theft. My wife and I graduated from high school in 1955 and 1956. We were both in college in the late '50s. True, we were in a liberal arts environment but nevertheless neither of us has any recollection of any discussion of, let alone technical information about, any computer in our high school or college experience.

As previously stated, the Monday after a Sunday graduation in 1959, I started employment with IBM in a two-month training class on punch card equipment. In Cleveland, at that time, the district included federal installations at NASA Lewis Research Center, the Navy Finance Center, several federal agency offices, and a couple of federal military depots. IBM was a major federal contractor, and the federal government was IBM's largest single customer. The federal team in the Cleveland District included a senior salesman, John Peterson; a senior systems engineer, Jack Hopler; a systems engineer, Wayne Senger, and a trainee—me. Initially as a trainee, I was not designated as technical support or sales support, so when an inquiry arrived from a military depot near Youngstown, I was sent to talk with the information supervisor and see what he wanted. I spent a few days in Youngstown helping the information systems supervisor run his month-end inventory reports and reviewed his other reporting requirements. He was using UNIVAC equipment so when I assisted him, I was learning directly our largest competitor's equipment and shortcomings. I returned to the Cleveland office and wrote up a proposal to provide IBM equipment to replace the UNIVAC gear and improve the reports while reducing the effort. The IBM senior sales engineer was skeptical. John did not think the Army would approve increasing monthly reporting expense in terms of equipment rental to improve their reporting and control as well as ease the effort of the system supervisor rather than add an assistant or two, perhaps from the service rather than civilian. The depot converted to IBM equipment that gave John his annual quota of net sales revenue increase. I was promoted to systems engineer and made a member of the federal team. Shortly thereafter, the Navy Finance Center committed to replace their IBM punch card equipment, a sizeable installation, with a then new IBM main frame model 7070 computer.

I split my time for a period, assisting the service and civilian personnel in processing the payroll for the entire US Navy, active duty and retired, while attending a customer training class learning how to program a 7070. There were no 7070s in existence, so we used the IBM 650 at the training center and subsequently the IBM 704 at NASA and then at the company datacenters in Chicago and New York until finally a 7070 was available in New York and later Chicago. This was in 1960 and 1961. I learned that a computer was this massive piece of electronics attended by rows of magnetic tape drives and one or two large electromechanical printing devices and usually a resident maintenance engineer. From a technical view, this device was capable of some limited overlapped processing, encompassing mostly tape record reading and writing, monitored by system interrupts and status registers. Our designated computer for delivery was serial number 10; however, we were the first delivery to the field. My role was to support Navy staff, primarily civilian, in writing, testing, and ultimately, executing file conversion from punched cards to magnetic tape. On our trips to New York and Chicago with Navy personnel, our now three-member team of system engineers supported all assignments from conversion to regular monthly, quarterly, and annual processing software requirements. It is my recollection that we did extensive testing in October and November, simulated an actual December year-end run and then initiated a three-month parallel processing protocol before cutting over to full time live payroll processing in April. I was one of five or so people in the Cleveland District who had actually written operating code for and laid hands on a big main frame computer by mid-1962.

In short order, several events occurred within IBM. The field operations of the federal systems group were discontinued, and all federal support was under the supervision of the Washington division. IBM announced the 1400 series of main frame computers, lower priced yet quite capable of being configured for major tasks. IBM started paying systems engineers salaries equal to or above the customer information systems managers and significantly above sales engineers' salaries but with none of the sales incentives. These circumstances led me to stay in technical support and become a manufacturing industry specialist. This turn of events resulted in my assignment in a support position on three major Cleveland organizations at the time: White Motor Company, Premier Industries, and the Weatherhead Company. As a result of the efforts of our industrial sales teams, all of these organizations became users of IBM 1400 systems supporting their applications, including general ledger accounting, inventory forecasting and control, standard cost accounting and payroll.

Over time, I moved on to Westinghouse Electric and the into the world of entrepreneurial technical sales of equipment and software. The entrepreneurial change in direction occurred after my application background shifted from information systems to industrial computer control. In the field of industrial control, the computer was connected to instruments that measured real time variables from the plant or process which the system supervised or monitored. This shift in my field of experience occurred during the late 1960s into 1970.

The IBM 7000 series of computers was the first generation of electronic systems not employing vacuum tubes as their fundamental computing element. Instead, this first generation employed diodes, resistors, transistors, and capacitors mounted on circuit boards coupled with ferrite donuts of magnetic memory and magnetic tapes and slowly rotating drum memories as the constituents of their computing power. This generation of computers consumed fantastic amounts of power, generated a good deal of heat, and frequently broke down requiring maintenance. In the '70s the mini-computer came on the scene represented by companies such as Digital Equipment Corporation (DEC), Data General, Prime Computer Systems, Modcomp, Charles River Data Systems, Point 4 and several others. Computers continued to get less expensive, more reliable, faster, and have greater memory capacity as well as tolerate real world temperature and humidity environments.

Information technology focused on processing vast amounts of data at regular intervals of days, weeks, months, and years . Industrial control processes real time information from instrumentation and responds in milliseconds to change speed, pressure, temperature, or position. As computer speed, reliability, and capacity continue to increase, computers are on a path to continue gathering more and more information about our desires and needs as well as anticipate the resources necessary to satisfy our physical comfort. Self-driving cars, automated "fulfillment centers" within two hours of every customer, prepared meals delivered to your home, automobiles assembled in plants with few or no workers, all of these future potentials are in some state of current presence. Credit bureaus monitor all financial activity and credit inquiry, justifying reduced foreclosures and thus reducing credit overhead costs. Demand monitoring can optimize power generation with power demand control. Improved communication systems enable remote real-time meetings and decision-making, enabling employees to operate anywhere geographically reducing pressure on increased urbanization. Electronic interconnection can reduce reliance on personal relationship and enable objective selection from a field of alternatives. Maybe God is not dead; maybe God is a computer.

I truly hope this is not the outcome but there are dangerous signals we can see today. Facebook is a social media utility that initially built a following enabling individuals to talk with their friends or friend's friends with facility. The vehicle was monetized with advertising and while it remains the most employed social media utility, other forms have sprung up with new features and fewer ads. One way to stay ahead of the competition was to use artificial intelligence to improve the product offering. Facebook put together a team to analyze messages, preferences, objections, and strong reactions in volume or depth of expression and use artificially developed paradigms to improve message content to desired audiences. This approach required computers to communicate with each other rapidly and directly with no issue of interpretation. The approach resulted in computers communicating directly, machine to machine, in an evolved language that humans could not decipher. Facebook discontinued the project once this ability for totally independent machine to machine interchange was disclosed.

Elon Musk, the well-known billionaire inventor, entrepreneur, electric car and space rocket manufacturer, has stated that artificial intelligence is "the most serious threat to the survival of the human race." Ironically, he at one time criticized Mark Zuckerberg, founder and CEO of Facebook, stating that he had discussions with Mark and found him to have only a "limited understanding" of the subject. Yet while Facebook terminated its AI project out of concern, Musk continues to invest and be directly involved in OpenAI and other ventures pursuing AI and its extensions into human experience.

All of our activity on computers, cell phones, land lines, and credit cards leave digital footprints so also our viewing habits and geographic motion. Electronic devices now have essentially infinite storage capacity and well-developed techniques to store and retrieve records for analysis and extraction of behavioral actions and predictions. Computers can now model humans collectively and often individually. Initially, and for the most part, contemporaneously, this ability to model and predict behavior has been employed commercially and particularly by advertising and promotion operations to increase sales. As electronics continue to decrease in size, execution time and cost and increase in reliability, efficient power usage and memory capacity they will become more and more involved in our daily living. Self-driving cars will take us where we want to go using the most efficient route, taking into consideration not only distance but also speed limits and dynamic traffic patterns. This application will save fuel, save time, and dramatically reduce accidents with resulting savings of property loss and lives lost. Truck drivers will no longer be required to deliver goods between cities. Unskilled labor will be readily replaced by robots. Ultimately, computer decision support can become computer decision-making with no human interference. Values will be automated, and that impact on humanity is difficult to project. Major labor segments will be unnecessary, subjective values could be replaced by predictable outcomes. Enforcement of societal legal norms is a last barrier, and machines could take on that task as they gain independent mobility and physical action.

What is of particular concern to me is the fact that the growth of the impact of information processing has occurred over such a short period. When my mother was born in 1897, Wilbur and Orville Wright had not yet flown the first heavier-than-air craft at Kitty Hawk. By the time of my mother's death in 1992, man had walked on the moon, a span of almost one hundred years. The total number of computers in the world, awkward and huge vacuum tube machines, was probably somewhere between fifty and one hundred in 1959. Today, fifty-eight years later, my wife and I use five computers in our home, not including our two smart phones, and there are at least another six or so microprocessors in each of our two cars. Physics has predicted the availability of a "quantum computer" within the decade. One definition of a quantum computer is a complete functional processor in ten atoms. Super miniaturization provides logic resolution in nanoseconds or less with no appreciable need for power. This speed and packaging enable the extension of computer data collection and physical reaction into every aspect of our existence.

Statistical evaluation and prediction were a new field of concentration getting significant attention and research funding in the 1950s. Now every election outcome is known as the polls close even when the outcome is as unexpected as our last presidential contest, when prescient forecasters were predicting early in the evening that the probability of unexpected results was high owing to the observable sweep of Republicans in local and congressional contests. Business plans and strategies are built on a combination of intuition and statistical forecasting. Intuition is acceptable for limited risk opportunities with potentially high payouts. Larger scope decisions usually require extensive statistical analysis and generally require independent verification before executives in large multinational corporations are ready to play "you bet your career" on significant policy shifts. Statistics used to be based on small random samples that were carefully defined to represent the larger universe of possibilities. Today, sample size can be limitless because of the impact of technology on communications and computing data storage and manipulation. The "black magic" of establishing a representative sample is less and less significant in building a statistically accurate representation of reality as it is experienced and thus as it will be experienced.

In the field of industrial control, predictive control was employed to preset mill stand settings for shaping metal and then almost instantaneous feedback was employed to make Vernier adjustments to produce on gauge material. Similarly, in refineries, local set point control is adjusted to adapt column operation as feedstock changes from one source to another while maintaining similar output profiles. Anticipatory control gets an operation close to desired production quickly with minimum loss of material, while usual closed loop control makes the necessary adjustments based on real time feedback to bring about total on specification production.

There is no greater visible demonstration of this phenomena than a traditional hot strip steel mill of the late 1960s reducing a white, hot ingot of metal in a rectangular cube with dimensions of approximately 3'x 4'x 12' to a continuous strip of sheet steel 80" wide, 1.5 to 2.0 millimeters thick and a half mile long. The white, hot metal ingot slams into the first stand with a huge shower of sparks and a felt vibration as the distorted ingot proceeds to the next mill stand where the elongated piece of metal accelerates toward yet the next reduction stand in a line of stands numbering up to almost twenty. All of this occurs as people watch but the computer, its motor operated control variables and feedback measurements of energy absorbed and speed from front end to back end of material, is automatically adjusted through thousands of independent variables stretching the mile or so of the entire operation.

In this example, the computer employs its database of known relationships, historically observed performance and current conditions, including temperatures, speeds, looper tensions and mill apertures, and continuously adjusts settings based on the values of finished goods it is targeted to produce. This same technique of feedback control to a supervisory set of desired specifications is employed in refineries, chemical plants, robotic manipulation of piece part production, and warehouse storage and retrieval systems. Part of the technology is the ability to measure variables and have their values available as needed, part of the technology includes defining the relationship of the measured variable to a controllable piece of equipment such as a valve, a motor, a pump, or a furnace or other heat source. This production control is equivalent to military tactics. Tactical superiority generally wins battles, and when tactical supcriority is combined with sound and executable strategy, the battle victories usually add up to winning the war. In manufacturing, winning the war includes finance, distribution, marketing, sales, and human resources in a unified strategy all affected by the validity of the information and its manipulation in support of the objective. Technology has enabled the availability of ever faster significant information to support business decision-making and continuously improve productivity yielding more from less.

All of this activity of gathering information, establishing rules of relationships, and then integrating the rules and information into a strategic whole is the art of mathematical modeling. The computer is programmed, or in the future, programs itself to build this set of data gathering and manipulation into equations representing physical activity and then directs controllable apparatus to bring to pass its desired outcome. When the goal is an objective and relatively easily defined point, such as produce economically lowest cost electricity from various possibilities given current demand on a network, then computers can do an admirable job of assaying alternatives and executing an optimum result. But what happens when computers are enabled to employ massive resources to determine optimum economic management for a society? Where does the innovative breakthrough that our society requires for its continued success and existence come from? What is the source of the saving "Black Swan", the event that occurs outside of the statistically predictable or historically observed chain of occurrence and is generally thought to be impossible, impractical, undesirable, or unlikely?

Does the computer network of the future decide what are the abilities of each or the needs of each? Does this network decide which task is important and what is each task worth? Do we each make our own decisions and accept responsibility for our own mistakes or is there an overarching plan whereby each of us has our assigned role? Do we collectively become totally predestined to the optimum values of machine logic? This possibility is a truly frightening prospect that is only offset by an alternative possibility of destruction in the event that weapons of mass destruction are available to irresponsible leaders in our segmented and divided world. These alternatives of future possibility make current situations much more tolerable and should drive the communities of believers to prayers for guidance either for divine intervention or the development of intelligent alternatives.

In the past, major advances, such as the agricultural revolution; the birth of awareness and knowledge; the industrial revolution; and even the atomic age, have come into our history with bold forecasts of doom and gloom that overlooked the accompanying advantages and some level of restraint that enabled social progress to outstrip threats to continued existence. I pray that the impact of new technology from the new quantum physics to new information manipulation to new genetic manipulation brings an ethic of positive restraint that only acts to improve humanity's existence.

Observations and Conclusions

I have written this chapter previously but determined that it needed reorganization and clarification. In retrospect, the discussions were not lacking germane points, but I was not satisfied that the presentation was fully developed as a theology reflecting a study of the history of faith as well as previously reviewing the development of personal faith and a reconciliation of religious faith and today's expanded scientific knowledge. Keeping in mind the daunting criteria this topic development implies, I will now attempt to describe my observations and conclusions that provide a coherent discussion of our Creator.

God's existence

Previously, I discussed the anthropic principle that rests on the observation that any deviation in numerous critical environmental ratios, some of which require parts per million plus or minus ten parts, would threaten the existence of intelligent life on earth. This thesis is often questioned on the basis of large numbers. If we now have observed or implied at least one hundred billion galaxies and each galaxy has several billions of stars, many of which have orbiting planets, isn't it inevitable that some quantity of planets with the same environmental conditions would exist within the cosmos?

This attack points to pure randomness to duplicate our survival conditions. Yet Paul Davies, an internationally awarded theoretical physicist, in *The Mind of God: The Scientific Basis for a Rational World* presents strong evidence that the universal mathematical nature of our cosmos suggests that human scientists discover the mathematical relationships of our cosmos that were present before we collectively discovered their existence. The central theme of this book questions why:

> We, who are children of the universe—animated stardust—can nevertheless reflect on the nature of that same universe, even to the extent of glimpsing the rules on which it runs... What does it mean? What is Man that we might be party to such privilege?... Through conscious beings the universe has generated self-awareness. This can be no trivial detail, no minor byproduct of mindless, purposeless forces. We are truly meant to be here.

In summary, I accept the conclusion of Dr. Davies, Dr. Polkinghorne, and a host of other scientists and academicians, including Dr. Francis Collins, that there is significant evidence to support the view that our existence is planned and has a purpose. If we are planned, this requires the presence of a p lanner who has designed our presence with some objective or purpose. If there is a creator, it strikes me that we should spend significant intellectual, physical, and emotional resources pursuing knowledge of his creation and his purpose.

God's nature

If I could reliably and unerringly define and explain the nature of God, I do not believe I would be sitting here at age eighty-five typing my thoughts in an as yet unpublished tome. What I can do is describe what I witness and how I interpret these "realities" as indications of the nature of God as reflected by his creation:

- dynamic. Creation is not static and permanent. It is dynamic with beginnings and endings. If it were to be static, there would be no renewal or rebirth since all to be created would have been created. There would be no death or termination, no birth or regeneration, and there would be little or no need for opposing forces, such as gravity and centrifugal force.
- acceptance. We all seem to need to be appreciated and desired. If this is a fundamental component of our being, presumably it would reflect a similar need by our Creator. If appreciation is a basic trait from God, free will is a requirement for creation. It is the consequence of choice that transmits value to options we consider necessary. Love, respect, and attention have value when they are elected. Conversely, these desired feelings in others diminish in value when they are evident only as obedience forced by threatened or evident disastrous alternatives.
- randomness. Randomness is a necessary ingredient in creation since it offers a non-judgmental contradiction to justice that makes justice a desirable characteristic worthy of striving for.
- love. It is consistent with my observations of parentage that God would send His Son to teach us how to survive in His creation. Love, service, and respect for our God and each other are the fundamental elements of the quality, and perhaps, even the possibility of our continued existence. Life could still be eternal somewhere in the cosmos even if we elected to behave badly enough to terminate life on earth.
- jesus. The existence of Jesus as a historical person is significantly probable given the records and eyewitnesses of the period. If Jesus existed as described in the New Testament, He either was who He said He was, or else He was a dangerous madman whose goal was not achieved and whose enduring influence is a con job of unbelievable proportions. If Jesus was real, and many have gone to

martyrdom attesting to His being and message, it would be of immense benefit to all of humanity to follow His call.
- presence. A creator god must exist in every corner of an unimaginably immense cosmos simultaneously. Light moves at a speed of approximately 186×10^3 miles per second. Therefore, in a year light travels (186,000) x (60X60X24X365) a distance of 586,569,600,000 miles. This represents a distance greater than circling the earth twenty-three million times! Our cosmos is currently estimated to include at least a hundred billion galaxies spanning billions of light years of separation. Our God is simultaneously here conversing individually with any of His 7.5 billion humans and billions of light years distant with potentially billions of other planets some of which might include their own large populations of self-aware creatures of God. I have trouble understanding this mathematical scope as a numerical expression let alone having any practical appreciation of the true scope of size, space, and quantity. Yet, He listens and speaks to me! What a dichotomy between the ego that makes Him personal and the humility that acknowledges that we are less than a grain of sand on an immense never-ending beach. I cannot understand how this is possible, but I know that this is the scope of our Creator and Designer, and there is significant witness-based evidence to support this conclusion inferentially, empirically, philosophically, and mathematically.
- competition. I have read quite a bit of C. S. Lewis and find myself usually agreeing with his observations. However, I have always had some difficulty accepting his conclusion that competition was mean and socialism, with ownership in common, seemed the best ethical and moral approach to governing. I could not differentiate Lewis's recommendation from the governing postulate of "from each according to his ability and to each according to his need," the governing rule of Engels and Marx. The

fundamental problem with this approach to governance is that it doesn't work. Administration requires a bureaucracy which leads to corruption. There has been an observable exception in some Anabaptist Hutterite communities particularly in the states of the Dakotas in the USA. It is my understanding from *The Anabaptist Story* by William R. Estep that the Hutterites developed communities and congregations limited to one hundred fifty persons, initiating a new community whenever the number exceeded one hundred fifty. In these communities, everyone shared ownership of all property, and individuals received what they needed from community resources. Others have noted that several primitive cultures seemed effective when limited to a quantity of one hundred fifty or so. This quantity seems a limit on individual familiarity whereby the community, as a whole, knows every individual and their circumstance without any requisite bureaucratic interpretation or interference. Apart from this efficiency of small communities with strong common values, nature seems dependent on competition as a driving force for survival even to the point of identifying natural selection as a primary evolutionary driver in species and cultures.

- free will. God has given us the privilege of being His partners exercising control over His world. As elaborated by Rabbi Harold Kushner, our ability to freely error in our judgements and decisions provides significant positive value to those occasions when we elect to do the correct and appropriate activity. This inherent freedom enables us to do great harm to ourselves and others. Free will also enables us to individually interpret and define religious ritual and observance even in the most liturgical, top down, systems of belief. Who among us has not observed the faithful congregant who personally varies in their behavior from the dogma of their religious affiliation?
- eternal. In my reading of microbiologists and theories of the origin of life, one description of being alive as a

state was that any organism that fights entropy was, by definition, alive. Further, there has been no successful demonstration of combining any inert chemicals in any controlled environment that created a cell that fought entropy. At this time, we can clone life from life, but we cannot create life. To me, this barrier speaks to the duality of living seeming to require both a material existence and a spiritual essence. I find it probable that life exists elsewhere among the billions of galaxies we have come to be aware of. Is life eternal? It seems to me, based on big numbers and statistical probability, life will continue into eternity somewhere in our cosmos. Is my life eternal? Not in its present form. If I am totally a materialist being, I believe my materialist form and identity cease except as residual components deposited in earth, wind, and water. But if we are composed as a dual organism, the spiritual component could continue in a form I cannot imagine.

The preceding are my observations and based upon the data I have gathered, either through direct experience or reading of the experiences of others.

Humanity's response

In summary, I have presented our experience of creation and existence to be the domain of God the Creator, including a dynamic environment with competition and free will, populated by humans who need approval and seek and receive love while constantly in His presence. In this creation, humanity's response to belief in God is religion, the organized recognition of our relationship to our God. As with every other human endeavor, religion is not a perfect structure or protocol for expressing worship.

- Written instruction. Torah and other Old Testament Books, Intertestamental Books such as the Apocrypha and Pseudepigrapha, Gnostic Gospels, New Testament Books, Qur'an, Book of Mormon and supporting libraries such as the Book of Common Prayer and *Science and Health with Key to the Scriptures* are all viewed by many of their followers as inerrant cannons of their faith authored or inspired by the Creator or the Creator's exclusive representative. I do not have reason to challenge the sincerity of the various human authors creating all or portions of the foregoing. Obviously, these documents have significant differences one from another and even differences and inconsistencies within various offerings. All of these canonical references are subject to interpretation and study usually led by clerical representatives of the various possible denominations. Dr. Diarmaid MacCulloch wrote *Christianity: The First Three Thousand Years*. The work is an historical approach to the development of the Christian church beginning with the preceding millennia of the Jewish faith. Among other points, MacCulloch itemizes how differing interpretations of the significance of different passages of the Bible or different rituals fractured the church into competing denominations that ofttimes had open conflict with fellow Christians of a different denomination as well as with other religious traditions they considered as spiritually inferior. In all cases the written word and even more so, its interpretation, was employed as a vehicle to provide exclusion.

- Hierarchical structure of churches. The early Christian church was a loose affiliation of the disciples of Jesus and their followers, primarily from among the middle eastern Jewish community. After the conversion of Saul and his subsequent evangelical mission to the gentiles, the Christian church became the first religious response to advocate a universal membership, and this new policy was sharply debated to eventually allow preaching to and including the uncircumcised. The next divisive distinction started to develop between the Latin-speaking church and the Greek-speaking and culturally-attached church. For some period, the ruler of the church was the Bishop of Rome. When Constantine recognized Christianity, he emphasized a "New Rome" Constantinople, the "capital" of the Eastern Church. Suddenly there were two competing heads of Christendom. As divisions and departures continued in "the church" most denominations initiated their primary clerical authority. It took centuries until the newer Protestant and Reformed churches developed representative councils and only relatively recently non-denominational evangelical structures. Until recently, church affiliation was a primary litmus test for legitimacy of persons seeking civil authority.

- secular materialism. Some credit Aristotle because of his emphasis on analysis, others Ibn al Haytham because of his emphasis on reproducibility, but certainly, by the time of Sir Isaac Newton, modern science had developed its roots. Modern science is built on a loosely defined scientific methodology of observe, hypothesize, predict, test, and evaluate. For some period, this approach, which yielded many breakthroughs in building knowledge of our physical universe, was projected as the only path to truth with respect to our existence. Carl Popper was an advocate of the approach that sought a singular evidence of a failed prediction as a demonstration of fallibilism thus proving incorrectness. In particular, he proposed that this search in a laboratory undercut any claim of truth by the humanities which could merely adjust hypothesis to extend conditions and define the exception as part of the observation. Yet as our exposure to quantum mechanics grew, we found that, among other conditions, truth seemed to vary by scale. The black or white equations of Newtonian physics did not always work, and in certain cases, probability was a determining factor in outcomes. Expanding understanding of the discoveries by Watson and Crick has also clouded the prior hypothesis of a tree of life emanating from a single living cell into all observed specie variations driven only by natural selection. Evolution is a factor, but mathematically, it does not satisfy the statistical challenge to exclusively produce billions of species, alive and extinct, within five hundred million years particularly given that nucleotide pairings randomly adjusted seem more likely to produce variations that do not survive reproduction or if surviving are not fecund.

Thus far, my theology has established my belief in the Creator and defined the nature of His creation. Further, I have delineated some of our responses to His gifts, including denial. There are physical characteristics of creation that are fundamental to its existence and can be threats to our existence. In most cases, we have the ability to manage these threats to minimize their negative impact. Our failure to appreciate the nature of the creation in which we live, whether through ignorance; or because we parse words to justify our bad behavior; or because we individually strive for personal power at any cost , cost us opportunities for greater realization of the positive potential of the creation He gave us. Many among us deny that observed limits on His benefits, as fostered by our behavior, is frequently a consequence of denying His being. Our world is not what it could be. But, if we accepted the major themes of love, respect, civility, concern, and caring as major elements of our daily conduct, while recognizing the system's limiting forces of competition and randomness, our world would surely be much improved. This summary of positive possibilities of belief is not a threat of damnation or a law of "Thou shalt nots" but rather a motivation for greater realization.

If my observations on the existence and nature of God have validity, there are still issues to consider such as corporate worship and prayer. Corporate worship is a reinforcing experience for believers and can be a method employed in evangelistic endeavors. Corporate worship is within the realm of religion and brings with it all of the negative aspects of organized religion, including amassing of wealth, politics and self-serving power accumulation. Organized religion also brings with it, rich assets of liturgical consistency, congregational administration, and spiritual study. Recently I encountered a minster whose charismatic personality and effective message successfully gave birth to a large non-denominational evangelical congregation and physical plant. After many years of operation and the support of many congregants, a difference developed between some members of the congregation and the minister resulting in the minister's departure. The absence of any denominational authority enabled this situation to develop into an irremediable confrontation with damage to all involved. An effective denomination provides a vehicle to resolve differences of this type. Organized worship also can engender a cumulative spiritual response among the total congregation greater than the sum of individual experiences. Most of us have experienced the strength of feeling brought about through the support of family and friends. That level of sometimes overwhelming emotional support is able to at least be duplicated in periods of corporate worship. The gathering of a worship community also provides scale to congregational outreach programs, such as homeless sheltering, addiction prevention and recovery, and sheltering and supporting abused children and women.

I have read recently of the growth of Christianity worldwide as well as the decline of all mainline Christian denominations in the USA. According to the statistics gathered by Pew Research, the growth is strongest in the southern hemisphere and Asia. Given present trends, China will have more Christians than the United States by 2030. Growth was characterized as primarily Pentecostal or Evangelical and in either case more oriented toward literal scriptural interpretation. South Korea was cited as having several congregations numbering ten thousand active members or more. While there have been examples in Africa, the United States, Korea and elsewhere of charismatic preachers with yachts, private airplanes, limousines and other luxuries, this picture of advantage enjoyed by clerical elite has not been the standard observed in the majority of cases. What has been generally observed in this growth of Christianity is a more scripture-based and emotional appeal to the marginalized communities, particularly in our southern hemisphere. This seems reminiscent of the era of tent revivals and fundamentalist crusades in a time when America's cultural environment was less sophisticated.

Thomas Sowell has stated that there are two types of people in the world: those who are visionary driven and those who are data driven. The book, *Future Faith*, by Wesley Granberg-Michaelson to my mind represents a visionary interpretation of current Christian statistics. The author points out the observed phenomena of growth in membership of Evangelical and Pentecostal churches in Asia, South America, and Africa, and while he expresses reservations about the literalist tendencies in these cases, he concludes that this emotion-driven approach in Asia and the southern hemisphere will require that Christianity, as experienced in the west and America in particular, has to be cleansed of the individualistic orientation as driven by the Enlightenment. Historically, in less sophisticated periods, the West experienced church growth as a consequence of massive and frequent revivalist movements only to see membership wane as time and events damped emotional enthusiasm. I pray for two outcomes: First, that the new convert enthusiasm prevails and grows; second, emotion driven belief is reinforced by reasonable analysis. It is my opinion that only a reasoned analysis of faith can prevail over time in a secular materialist world of technology and scientific progression. Recently, a priest commented on the loss of Notre Dame Cathedral that "church is where the faithful go to recover their strength." Christianity needs growth and strength as found in abundant corporate worship.

The issue of prayer and miracles is another area where faith is often challenged. John Shelby Spong, an Episcopal bishop, points out that much of our praying is petitioning God for our requests much like a child petitions Santa Claus. In his book, *Unbelievable*, Spong also questions the incarnation and resurrection of Jesus, so it does seem he has some difficulty accepting Christianity, which he says he professes. I agree that oft repeated creeds, prayers, and dogmas are of limited value in bona fide exercises of faith. This does not translate into prayer having no value or miracles not existing. We are all, after some degree of maturation, aware of unanswered prayer and the sometimes long- term positive outcome resulting from unanswered prayers. Judges on earth, who have jurisdiction of only a defined orbit, grant or decline pleas based on their knowledge of the law and experience in its efficacy and limits of application. Consider God hearing pleas of eight billion souls sometimes in direct contradiction between one and another. Consider God hearing pleas of self-desired outcomes that might indirectly cause harm to others. This is not to argue that unanswered prayer is a desired result of a prayer of petition but to point out that sometimes the reason for declining a desired outcome might be knowledge of a broader knowledge base. Sometimes, in the experience of millions of individuals over thousands of years, prayers of petition are answered or at least seemingly answered. I know of no statistical database on the outcomes of prayers of petition.

Like many other authors, ministers, congregants, and non-believers, I have my opinion or understanding of our Creator and our relationship with Him. I know there are many who might regard my positions as heretical or worse, but I find personal comfort in what I believe is an examined, reasonable, and demonstrable relationship with our Creator and His only begotten son. I trust that those who have read thus far will also find reason and comfort in my views.

Bibliography

Breyer, Stephen. *The Court and the World.* New York: Vintage Books. 2016

Brueggemann, Walter. *Theology of the Old Testament.* Minneapolis: Fortress Press. 1997

Davies, Paul *The Mind of God: The Scientific Basis for a Rational World.* New York: Simon & Schuster 2005

Diamond, Jared. *The World Until Yesterday: What Can We Learn from Traditional Societies?* New York: Penguin Group (USA). 2012

Estep, William R. *The Anabaptist Story: An Introduction to Sixteenth-Century Anabaptism.* Grand Rapids: William B Eedermans Publishing Company. Third Edition 1996

Granberg-Michaelson, Wesley. *Future Faith (Word & World)* Minneapolis: Fortress Press. 2018

Gribbin, John & Mary. *In Search of Schrodinger's Cat: Quantum Physics and Reality.* New York: Bantam Books. 1984

Harari, Yuval Noah. *Sapiens: A Brief History of Human Kind.* New York: Harper Collins Publishers Inc. 2014

Lane, Nick. *The Vital Questions.* New York: WW Norton & Company. 2016

Macculloch, Darmaid. *Christianity: The First Three Thousand Years.* New York: Penguin Group (USA) Inc. 2010

Morgan, Gary R. *Understanding World Religions in 15 Minutes a Day* Bloomington: Bethany House Publishers. 2012

Spong, John Shelby. *Unbelievable: Why Neither Ancient Creeds Nor the Reformation Can Produce a Living Faith Today.* HarperOne, 2018

www.ingramcontent.com/pod-product-compliance
Lightning Source LLC
LaVergne TN
LVHW011737060526
838200LV00051B/3207